Crock Pot F

The Top 100 Best Slow Cooker Recipes Of All Time

By Ace McCloud
Copyright © 2016

Disclaimer

The information provided in this book is designed to provide helpful information on the subjects discussed. This book is not meant to be used, nor should it be used, to diagnose or treat any medical condition. For diagnosis or treatment of any medical problem, consult your own physician. The publisher and author are not responsible for any specific health or allergy needs that may require medical supervision and are not liable for any damages or negative consequences from any treatment, action, application or preparation, to any person reading or following the information in this book. Any references included are provided for informational purposes only. Readers should be aware that any websites or links listed in this book may change.

Table of Contents

Introduction 5

Chapter 1: Top 10 Best Beef and Lamb Recipes 7

Chapter 2: Top 10 Best Chicken and Pork Recipes 15

Chapter 3: Top 10 Best Seafood Recipes 23

Chapter 4: Top 10 Best Soup and Stew Recipes 30

Chapter 5: Top 10 Best Vegetarian Recipes 38

Chapter 6: Top 10 Best Pasta and Grain Recipes 47

Chapter 7: Top 10 Best Sauce and Condiment Recipes 55

Chapter 8: Top 10 Best Breakfast and Lunch Recipes .62

Chapter 9: Top 10 Best Appetizer Recipes 69

Chapter 10: Top 10 Best Deserts and Treats 75

Conclusion 83

My Other Books and Audio Books 84

Be sure to check out my website for all my Books and Audio books.
www.AcesEbooks.com

Introduction

I want to thank you and congratulate you for buying the book, "Crock Pot Recipes; The Top 100 Best Slow Cooker Recipes of All Time."

This book contains proven steps and strategies on how to make delicious meals while you are out that your family will love.

Slow Cookers or Crock Pots are a real help to families where parents work a full time job. Mom or Dad may not get home until 5 or 6 o'clock and a good meal may take an hour or more to prepare. When dinner has been cooking all day in the crock pot, the family can make a salad or side and be sitting down to dinner in just a matter of minutes. Meals are not just regular meals when they are cooked in a slow cooker. The food cooks very slowly for about 8 hours, so everything melds together nicely and melts in the mouth. Once you start cooking in a crock pot, it is hard to go back to cooking in an oven or on top of the stove because food is so delicious and it is so easy to do. Using a crock pot helps save money and eat healthy. No more running out for expensive take out and you are less likely to stop on the way home for pizza, burgers or other fast food that add calories and fat to your diet.

Slow cookers and crock pots are the same thing. What they are called depends on the manufacturer. The pot part is made from a heavy stoneware that resembles an old fashion crock used way back in the pioneer days. People would salt meat in crocks, they would pickle meats and vegetables and store butter. The reason a crock was so good for this was because it helped the contents stay cool. When heat is applied to a crock, it makes the contents hot. The stoneware retains heat and distributes it to make whatever is being cooked inside cook evenly.

The stoneware pot fits into a metal out vessel and inside, on the base and sometimes up the sides, is a heating element that runs with electricity. A crock pot has a knob on the outside where you set the heat to high, low or warm and sometimes they even have some vent holes. The lid of a crock pot is usually made of heavy glass that fits lightly over the crock into a grove to keep it tight. A slow cooker will not work properly without the lid. The lid keeps heat in the crock so the food cooks and liquids stay in the crock instead of evaporating into the air. That is why everything is so delicious and juicy when cooked in a slow cooker.

The food is put in the crock pot, sometimes just dumped all in together and sometimes layered. It is then turned on in the morning and set to low for 8 or more hours or high for 4 or less hours. Some slow cookers even have a timer and you can set it to cook for the proper amount of time and then go to warm all by itself. The heat starts in the base of the vessel and flows up the sides cooking the food somewhat like using a Dutch Oven on a stove under low heat. The big difference between a slow cooker and Dutch Oven is that the crock pot doesn't need to be watched or stirred. Turn it on and leave for work without worrying because it doesn't get hot enough to burn the food. That is not something you can do with a pot on the stove.

The following is a great video entitled "Tips for Cooking in a Slow Cooker" from Dummies.com. This tells you how much liquid to include and how to make food look and taste very good.

Slow cookers come in many shapes and sizes. Large oblong ones are good for large families and can cook whole chickens or roasts. The regular sized round crock pot hold enough for a family, but the contents may have to be chopped up to fit. There are even small crock pots big enough for one or two people.

The nice thing about crock pots is that you can cook anything in them. Main dishes, soups, sides and even dessert cooks up in a slow cooker. Most common recipes can be converted to crock pot recipes. Remember that liquid does not evaporate in a crock pot like it does on the stove, so you must adjust by only adding half the liquid called for in the regular recipe. If it says to use 4 cups of chicken stock, use only two unless you are cooking beans, rice or pasta that soaks up the liquid.

The following are 100 delicious, mouth-watering recipes for a crock pot that should make great dinners for working families. They include main dishes, soups and stews, pastas, breakfast and lunch ideas, appetizers and even desserts. Let's start our journey on a new way of cooking that makes delectable recipes that are nutritious and easy to make.

Chapter 1: Top 10 Best Beef and Lamb Recipes

Some cuts of beef and lamb tend to be a little tough, but when you cook them in a crock pot for several hours, they melt in your mouth. The slow cooking makes the meat very tender and delicious. You can cook a whole leg of lamb in a crock pot or you might opt for a homey pot roast recipe. You can make fillings for sandwiches or something exotic with lots of spice and curry.

Eye of Round Roast and Vegetables
This recipe only takes a short amount of time to prepare and will be ready in 8 hours when you get home from work. Either prepare it the night before and just plug it in before work or dice the vegetables in the morning.

Ingredients:
1 teaspoon oregano
1 teaspoon paprika
1 teaspoon garlic powder
1 teaspoon dried onion powder
1/2 teaspoon salt
1 teaspoon ground pepper
1 – 3 to 4 pound eye of round roast
6 to 8 red potatoes quartered (do not remove skin)
3/4 cup baby carrots (more if you like carrots)
2 stalks of diced celery
1 whole onion, diced
1 – 1.2 ounce package of dry beef gravy mix
1 tablespoon flour
1-1/2 cup beef broth

Directions:
1. In a small bowl combine the oregano, paprika, garlic and onion powder, salt and pepper and mix well. Rub the roast with the combination and set it aside. You can do this overnight, wrap the roast in plastic wrap and refrigerate overnight.
2. After spraying the crock with nonstick spray, layer in the potatoes, carrots, celery and onions and place the roast on top.
3. In a large glass measuring cup, whisk together the beef broth and dry gravy mix and poor it on the sides of the roast.
4. Cook low for 8 hours or on high for 5 hours. Remove the roast and set it on a platter for cutting after about 5 minutes of sitting. Remove the vegetables with a slotted spoon and place in a bowl.
5. Add the flour and whisk until the gravy thickens and serve on the side in a gravy boat.

Note: Instead of using just beef broth only use 1 cup and add 1/2 cup of a good red wine.

Italian Pot Roast

This pot roast has an Italian flavor with fennel and tomato sauce that you can use to top a little bit of pasta on the side. The meat just melts in your mouth and it only takes about 20 minutes to prepare and 9 to 11 hours on low and about 5 hours on high to make.

Ingredients:
1 teaspoon toasted and crushed fennel seed
1 teaspoon garlic powder
1/2 teaspoon pepper
2-1/2 pound boneless beef pot roast
2 trimmed and cored fennel bulbs cut thin
3 chopped carrots
1 peeled and thin cut onion
26 ounce jar tomato pasta sauce
1/4 cup fresh chopped Italian parsley

Directions:
1. Place fennel seed on foil covered pan sprayed with a nonstick spray and place under the broiler just long enough to toast them. Crush with a mortar and pestle. Place in a small bowl with the garlic powder and pepper to make a rub.
2. Trim the fat from the roast and rub the above ingredients on all sides. Refrigerate overnight if starting the roast in the morning.
3. Place the sliced fennel, carrot and onion in the bottom of a non-stick sprayed crock pot and top with the roast. Cut the roast to fit if necessary.
4. Pour the tomato pasta sauce over top. Use a commercial brand or your own as long as it is about 26 ounces.
5. Cover and cook 9 to 10 hours on low or 5 hours on high.
6. Remove the roast and cut into pieces. Remove the vegetables with a slotted spoon to serve with the roast.
7. Cook up some penne or rigatoni, drain and use the sauce in the crock pot to put over top.

Old Fashion Tasting Salisbury Steak in a Slow Cooker

This recipe might taste old fashion, but you don't have to sweat over the stove for hours making it like you normally would. You don't even have to worry about making your own gravy because the ingredients take care of that for you. You do have to make the extra step of browning the patties, once you make them or they will not look very appetizing, but it only takes a few minutes on each side to do it. Just a note on using ground beef in a slow cooker. Use the leanest ground beef available and no less than 80%, otherwise, the excess grease will stay in the slow cooker and make the food greasy.

Ingredients:
1 package onion soup mix

1/2 cup bread crumbs
1 teaspoon garlic powder
1 egg
1/4 cup milk
2 pounds ground beef
1 tablespoon butter
1 large sweet onion, sliced thin
2 to 3 tablespoons flour
2 cans cream of mushroom soup mix
1/4 cup beef broth

Directions:
1. Place the soup mix, bread crumbs, garlic powder, egg and milk in a large bowl and stir to mix well. Add the ground beef and mix in with your hands making sure it is well combined. Form 8 patties set aside.
2. In a skillet, heat the butter until melted and sauté the onion until it is brown. Remove the onion from the skillet and set aside.
3. Dredge the patties in the flour lightly and brown on each side just enough to brown them, but not to cook through. Put them in a slow cooker that has been sprayed with non-stick spray.
4. Layer the onions on top in the crock pot.
5. In a 4 cup measuring cup whisk the cream of mushroom soup and the beef broth. Pour this over top of the patties.
6. Cook on low for 6 hours and serve with mashed potatoes.

Crock Pot Meatloaf
Yes, you can make meatloaf in a crock pot. It is best to have one of the larger pots that is oblong because you will be making two loaves that will sit side by side long ways. Again, use no less than 80% lean ground beef or you will have to deal with a great deal of grease.

Ingredients
2/3 cup unseasoned bread crumbs
1 tablespoon garlic powder
1/2 onion that has been peeled and chopped small
1 teaspoon salt
1 teaspoon pepper
1 teaspoon dried Italian seasoning herbs
2 eggs
1/2 cup milk
1-1/2 pound ground beef
1 cup Ketchup
1 tablespoon Worcestershire Sauce

Directions:

1. Mix together in a large bowl the bread crumbs, garlic powder, onion, salt pepper, Italian Seasoning, eggs and milk. Mix well and add the ground beef.
2. Use your hands to knead in all together and shape into two loaves. Place in the bottom of a non-stick sprayed oblong crock pot.
3. In a 4 cup measuring cup, whisk the ketchup and Worcestershire sauce and pour over the meatloaves.
4. Cook on low for 8 to 10 hours. Carefully remove loaves from the crock pot and serve. I always have a hard time getting them out of the crock pot without them breaking up, so I usually cut them in slices in the crock pot and take the slices out with a cake server or spatula.

Instead of using ketchup, cover with barbecue sauce and omit the Worcestershire sauce.

Slow Cooker Stroganoff
Stroganoff is a rich meal that is served over egg noodles. Round steak is usually a little tough, but when cooked in a slow cooker, it becomes very tender and delicious.

Ingredients:
1 – 1 pound round steak about 1 inch thick trimmed of fat
1 teaspoon olive oil
2 tablespoons minced garlic
1 medium peeled and sliced thin sweet onion
1/2 teaspoon salt
1/2 teaspoon pepper
1 teaspoon dried parsley
1 teaspoon paprika
1/3 cup flour
1 cup beef broth
2 cups sliced mushrooms
1 – 8 ounce container of sour cream
2 cups cooked egg noodles

Directions:
1. Cut the steak in diagonal strips and brown in a skillet with the olive oil and garlic. Place in the crock pot that has been sprayed with nonstick spray.
2. Layer in the onion, salt, pepper, and parsley. Place the browned strips on top.
3. In a small bowl, whisk together the paprika, flour and beef broth and pour over top. Place the lid on and cook for 8 hours on low. During the last half hour of cooking add the mushrooms and turn up to high.
4. Right before serving add the sour cream and stir well. Wait about 10 minutes and ladle the beef mixture onto steaming hot egg noodles and serve.

Corned Beef, Cabbage and Potatoes

I love to serve corned beef on St. Patrick's Day, but this recipe is good any time of year. The corned beef brisket always comes out falling apart before you can get it to the platter and it tastes beyond compare.

Ingredients
1 to 2 cups baby carrots
6 medium red potatoes, skins on, cut in quarters
2 medium peeled and sliced onions
1 – 3 to 4 pound corned beef brisket
1 bay leaf
1 can of beer
1 small cabbage that has been cut in wedges

Directions:

1. Spray the crock pot with non-stick spray. Place the carrots, potatoes, onions and bay leaf in the bottom.
2. Trim some of the fat off the brisket and lay it on top
3. Pour the beer over top and cook on low for 8 to 9 hours
4. The last 45 minutes of cooking, turn to high and add the cabbage wedges.
5. Remove the cabbage and place in a bowl. Remove the brisket and cut against the grain, if you can and it doesn't fall apart. Take the potatoes, carrots and onions out and put them with the cabbage to serve but find the bay leaf and remove it.

Leg of Lamb Off the Bone Crockpot Style

This lamb comes out delectable and falling off the bone and it is a little spicy with cumin, cinnamon and ginger. Because a whole leg of lamb would never fit in a crock pot, the recipe calls for a lamb shoulder cut in pieces. Serve for special occasions or any time you feel like making something special. Serve with some couscous and you have a meal fit for a king.

Ingredients:

1 cup baby carrots
1 medium peeled and chopped yellow onion
2 peeled and chopped cloves of garlic
1/2 cup halved dried apricots
1 teaspoon paprika
1 teaspoon ground cumin
1/2 teaspoon ground cinnamon
1/2 teaspoon ground ginger
2 tablespoons flour
1/4 teaspoon salt
1/2 teaspoon pepper
1-1/2 pound lamb shoulder

1/2 cup vegetable stock

Directions:
1. Spray the crock pot with non-stick spray and layer in the carrots, onion, garlic, apricots, spices, flour, salt and pepper.
2. Trim the fat off the lamb shoulder and cut it into 1 inch pieces. Place the pieces in the crock pot.
3. Pour the vegetable stock over top.
4. Place the lid on the crock pot and set on low for 5 hours and high for 8 hours. Serve over top couscous.

Slow Cooker Lamb Chops
This recipe only takes about 10 minutes to prepare, so it is easy to do in the morning before leaving for work. Just have everything out and ready to go. It will smell so good when you get home from work, resistance will be futile, but why would you want to resist?

Ingredients:
1 teaspoon oregano
1/2 teaspoon thyme
1 teaspoon garlic powder
1 teaspoon onion powder
1/4 teaspoon salt
1/8 teaspoon pepper
8 lamb chops
1 medium peeled and chopped yellow or sweet onion
2 minced cloves of garlic

Directions:
1. Mix together the herbs, salt and pepper and rub it into the lamb chops.
2. Place onion in the bottom the slow cooker that has been sprayed with nonstick spray and place the chops on top. Sprinkle the garlic over top
3. Cover and cook on low for 4 to 5 hours. Do not cook on high at all as there is no moisture added to this recipe.

Crock Pot Braised Lamb Shanks
The meat just falls of the bone when this recipe is finished stewing in the crock pot for a while. Serve with buttered egg noodles or mashed potatoes. The sauce is incredible and if there is any leftover without any lamb shanks left, you will want to sop it up with some extra bread.

Ingredients:
2 peeled and diced carrots
2 stalks of celery diced
1 medium peeled and diced yellow onion
1 – 14.5 ounce can of crushed tomatoes
2 tablespoons tomato paste

2 crushed cloves of garlic
1 teaspoon fresh thyme chopped
1 bay leaf
2 cups chicken stock
4 lamb shanks trimmed of fat
salt and pepper to taste
2 tablespoons olive oil
1 cup red wine

Directions:
1. Spray the crock with nonstick spray and put in the carrots, celery, onion, crushed tomatoes and tomato paste. Add the garlic and herbs and pour the stock over top. Stir gently to combine well.
2. Season the shanks with the salt and pepper. Heat a sauté pan to medium heat and add the olive oil until it gets very hot. Add shanks and brown on all sides. This should take about 5 minutes. Place the browned shanks in the slow cooker.
3. Remove the hot pan from the heat and pour in the wine. Turn the heat back on to medium high and simmer the wine stirring to get all the brown bits incorporated and pour into the crock pot.
4. Cover and cook on high 6 hours.
5. Remove shanks to a platter.
6. Take the bay leaf out of the sauce and use a stick blender to puree the sauce in the crock pot until smooth. Serve the sauce with the shanks.

Curried Lamb
If you like middle eastern flavors, this lamb is for you. There is one ingredient you can leave out if you want and that is the saffron since it is really expensive. Just using turmeric will give the dish the flavor needed, it would just be more pronounced with the saffron. Serve this lamb recipe over top some brown basmati rice and you have a meal you won't soon forget.

Ingredients:
1-14 ounce can of coconut milk
2 teaspoons coriander
1-1/2 teaspoons cumin
1 teaspoon turmeric
1 tablespoon paprika
1-1/2 tablespoons grated fresh ginger
1/8 teaspoon saffron threads
1-14 ounce can diced tomatoes
1/2 teaspoon salt
1 teaspoon pepper
2 tablespoons olive oil
3 peeled and minced cloves of garlic
4 pounds of lamb stew meat
Plain yogurt for garnish

Directions:
1. Pour the coconut milk into a sauce pan and add the coriander, cumin, turmeric, paprika, ginger and saffron threads, if using. Stir occasionally over medium heat until the mixture is smooth, creamy and steaming for around 5 minutes.
2. Spray crock pot with nonstick spray and pour the coconut milk in. Add the diced tomatoes salt and pepper to the crock pot.
3. Heat oil in a skillet and add the garlic. Sauté and add the stew meat browning lightly on all sides. Pour this into the crock pot and set it at low setting with the lid on for 8 hours.
4. Remove the lid and stir. Lower to the high setting and leave the lid off for half an hour to an hour. This dish has a great deal of liquid and leaving the lid off helps the liquid to thicken.
5. Serve over rice and top with plain yogurt.

Chapter 2: Top 10 Best Chicken and Pork Recipes

Chicken and pork do very well in a slow cooker and they come out tender and juicy every time. This chapter has delicious chicken recipes from a full roast chicken to old time chicken a biscuits and some Chinese cashew chicken. The pork recipes include pulled pork, several roasts, chops and ham recipes. Your family will appreciate sitting down at the dinner table right after coming home for these dinners.

Roast Whole Chicken
This recipe requires a large crock pot because you put the entire chicken in, bones and all. You place it upside down with the breasts against the bottom of the crock pot so that it cooks evenly.

Ingredients:
1 large peeled onion cut into wedges
1 teaspoon salt
1/4 teaspoon pepper
1/2 teaspoon garlic powder
1 teaspoon onion powder
1/4 teaspoon cayenne pepper
2 teaspoons paprika
1 teaspoon dried thyme
1 – 4 pound whole chicken

Directions:
1. Place the onion wedges at the bottom of the nonstick sprayed crock.
2. Combine the salt, pepper, garlic powder, onion powder, cayenne, paprika and thyme in a small bowel.
3. Remove any giblets from inside the cavity of the chicken. (If you want to chop and sauté them, then put them back in the cavity, you can.) Rub the outside and inside cavity with the spice rub in the bowl. Get some up under the skin on the breasts and thighs.
4. Turn the chicken upside down and place it breast down on top of the onions. Cook high 4 hours or low for 7 hours. The chicken will fall of the bone when it is done.

Lemon Chicken
This recipe is good enough for company. The chicken falls off the bone when done. The citrus flavor is not over powering, but very refreshing and delicious. You do have to do some browning and cooking on the stove for this recipe, but it is well worth the extra effort.

Ingredients:
1 – 3 pound whole chicken (cut in pieces)

1/2 teaspoon salt, or to taste
1/4 teaspoon pepper
2 tablespoons unsalted butter
2 cloves garlic, peeled and minced
3/4 teaspoon dried rosemary that has been crumbled
1 teaspoon dried oregano that has been crumbled
1/4 cup sherry or chicken broth
1/4 cup fresh squeezed lemon juice (about 2 to 3 lemons)

Directions:
1. Season the chicken pieces with salt and pepper.
2. Melt the butter in a sauté pan and add the minced garlic. Sauté for 2 minutes over medium heat and add the oregano and rosemary.
3. Brown the chicken pieces in the sauté pan, placing them in the bottom of nonstick sprayed crock pot when they are brown.
4. Add the sherry or broth to the frying pan and scrape all the brown bits from the pan. Pour this over top of the chicken in the crock pot. The lemon juice is added much later.
5. Cook on low for 7 hours. Add the lemon juice and cook on low another hour or turn up to high and cook for 20 more minutes. Skim any fat from the juices and serve with the chicken.

Cranberry Glazed Chicken in the Slow Cooker
Cranberry sauce tastes great with turkey and you can substitute turkey cutlets in this recipe. Cranberry sauce also goes well with chicken. It has a sweet and tart flavor that is very pleasing and fresh because of the cranberry sauce and the addition of your favorite bottled barbecue sauce. Use whole cranberry sauce for better results, but if you only have the jellied type, it can be used too. Also use boneless chicken breasts or turkey cutlets and serve with mashed potatoes.

Ingredients:
1 medium peeled and diced yellow onion
4 chicken breast halves
1/2 teaspoon salt
1 cup barbecue sauce
1 – 14 ounce can whole cranberry sauce
1/2 teaspoon dried thyme
1/2 teaspoon ground ginger
1/4 teaspoon pepper

Directions:
1. Place the diced onions in the bottom of a nonstick sprayed slow cooker.
2. Place the chicken breasts over top and sprinkle with salt. Brown them first in a little butter or oil if desired.
3. Pour the barbecue sauce over top of the chicken and dump the cranberry sauce over top.
4. Sprinkle with thyme, ginger and pepper

5. Cook low for 7 to 8 hours or on high for 4 or 5 hours.
6. Remove chicken breasts and ladle cranberry sauce over top of them and mashed potatoes.

Crock Pot Chicken and Biscuits
Chicken and biscuits is an old recipe where the chicken and vegetables are stewed carefully for a long time. The danger was that they would stick to the bottom of the pot and burn, so you had to keep stirring it while it cooked. You don't have to do that with a crock pot. Just turn it on, leave for work and dinner will almost be ready when you get home. Use chicken thighs if you like dark meat, but you can also make this with chicken breasts or a mixture of both.

Ingredients:
1 cup baby carrots
1 small peeled and chopped yellow onion
2 stalks sliced celery
3/4 cup flour
1/4 teaspoon parsley
1/8 teaspoon thyme
1/8 teaspoon sage
1/8 teaspoon rosemary
1/4 teaspoon salt
1/4 teaspoon pepper
1 – 1/2 pounds skinless chicken
1/2 cup white wine
1/2 cup chicken broth (or omit wine and use 1 cup chicken broth)
6 baking powder biscuits (make from dry biscuit mix and milk in the oven)
1 cup frozen peas
1/2 cup heavy cream
1/2 teaspoon more of salt
1/4 teaspoon more of pepper

Directions:
1. Toss the carrots, onion and celery with flour and place in a crock pot sprayed with nonstick spray.
2. Mix together the parsley, thyme, sage, rosemary, salt and pepper.
3. Place chicken on top of the vegetables and season well with the herb, salt and pepper mixture.
4. Pour the wine and broth around the sides. Cover and cook on low 5 to 6 hours or on high 2 – 1/2 to 3 hours.
5. About 15 minutes before done, mix up some baking powder biscuits from a biscuit mix and put them in the oven to bake. You can also use the flaky biscuits in a can.
6. About 10 minutes before done put the peas in the crock pot. They should be still frozen. Add the cream, salt and pepper. Stir to combine and cover.
7. Cut the baked biscuits in half and put the bottom in a bowl. Ladle out the chicken mixture over top and top with the top of the biscuit.

Easy Chinese (sort of) Cashew Chicken

This is an easy way to make cashew chicken without any fuss. You use mushroom soup, chicken tenders, and frozen Asian vegetables instead of making everything from scratch and it tastes pretty good and only takes about 10 minutes of preparation time.

Ingredients:
1 – 10 3/4 ounce can of golden mushroom soup
2 – 1/2 teaspoons low salt soy sauce
2 teaspoons fresh shredded ginger or 1 teaspoon dry ground ginger
1/4 teaspoon salt
1/4 teaspoon pepper
1-1/2 pounds chicken tenders
1 – 16 ounce package of frozen Asian vegetables (also called stir fry vegetables)
1 – 4 ounce can sliced mushrooms that has been drained
3/4 cup whole or halved cashews
Cooked brown or white rice

Directions
1. Spray the crock with nonstick spray.
2. Pour in the soup, soy sauce, ginger, salt and pepper.
3. Place the chicken on top and pour the frozen vegetables and canned mushrooms over top.
4. Place cover on and cook on low 6 to 8 hours or high 3 to 4 hours.
5. Before serving, pour the cashews in and mix. Serve over hot rice.

Pork Roast with Tasty Gravy

This pork roast will get your lips smacking it is so delicious and tender. It is seasoned with just one whole clove and you will be surprised at the flavor that 1 clove gives it, just fish it and the bay leaf out before serving. I usually stick the clove in the roast in the middle and pull it out before slicing. It doesn't really taste like there is cloves in the roast. It just gives it an extra oomph and brightness that is quite nice on the palate

Ingredients
1/2 teaspoon salt
1/4 teaspoon pepper
1 – 4 to 5 pound loin end roast
1 clove peeled and sliced garlic
1 tablespoon olive oil
2 medium sweet or yellow onions, sliced thin
1 bay leaf
1 whole clove
1 cup hot water
2 tablespoons Worcestershire sauce
2 tablespoons cold water

2 tablespoons cornstarch

Directions:
1. Rub the roast with the salt and pepper.
2. Cut slits in the top of the roast and insert slices of garlic all around
3. Place the olive oil in a hot skilled and brown the roast on all sides
4. Put one of the sliced onions in the bottom of a crock pot that has been sprayed with nonstick spray
5. Put the browned roast on top and top with the other onion and add the bay leaf and insert the clove.
6. Mix the hot water in a large measuring cup with the Worcestershire sauce and pour around the sides of the roast.
7. Cook 1 hour on high and turn to low for 9 to 10 hours longer
8. Remove the roast and onions from the crock pot and set aside. Remove the clove and bay leaf and throw those away.
9. In a bowl mix the cold water and cornstarch until it forms a smooth paste. Put the crock pot on high and whisk the paste into the liquid in the crock pot. Place the lid on and let it come to a boil and thicken into a lovely gravy This will take about 10 to 15 more minutes.
10. Slice the roast after 10 minutes of resting and serve with the gravy.

New Years' Pork Roast with Kielbasa and Sauerkraut

You can serve this any time of year, but it is especially good on New Year's Day to ensure a good year. You just turn the crock pot on and let it go. No other fuss is needed. It takes about 15 minutes to prepare and you are free to enjoy the festivities. Make mashed potatoes to serve with this feast.

Ingredients:
1 – 2 pound boneless pork loin roast
2 tablespoons olive oil

1/2 teaspoon salt
1/4 teaspoon pepper
3 sprigs of fresh thyme
4 pounds sauerkraut
1 pound kielbasa that has been cut into coins (small pieces)

Directions:
1. Preheat your oven broiler to high and place the roast in a roasting pan.
2. Brush the roast with olive oil and sprinkle with salt and pepper.
3. Place under the broiler for about 10 minutes or until the roast is browned.
4. Place half of the sauerkraut in a nonstick sprayed crock pot and place the browned roast in the middle with the thyme sprigs on top.
5. Place the pieces of kielbasa around the edges of the crock pot encircling the roast.
6. Cover with the rest of the sauerkraut and cook on high for 6 hours.

Note: I use the sauerkraut in the bag. There is some liquid to it that is needed in cooking the roast, but not as much as what is in cans. The bagged sauerkraut as a fresher flavor too.

Pork Chops and Gravy

These chops will melt in your mouth and literally fall of the bone. The gravy is delicious and does well or mashed potatoes. Serve with coleslaw and you have a great dinner.

Ingredients:
1/2 cup flour
1/2 teaspoon dry ground mustard
1/2 teaspoon garlic powder
1/2 teaspoon salt
1/4 teaspoon pepper
4 bone in pork chops about 1/2 to 1 inch thick
2 tablespoons olive oil
1/4 cup more flour
1 can (14.5 ounce) chicken broth

Directions:
1. Combine the 1/2 cup flour, mustard, garlic powder, salt and pepper in a re-closable plastic bag. Add chops, one at a time, and shake in order to coat each with the flour mixture.
2. Heat a skillet to medium high and add the olive oil. Add the chops and brown on both sides.
3. Place the chops in a non-stick sprayed slow cooker crock.
4. Pour the 1/4 cup flour into a bowl and whisk it until smooth with the chicken broth. Pour around the chops in the slow cooker.
5. Cover and cook on low 3 to 4 hours. The meat should be tender.
6. Remove the chops to a serving plate and keep warm in a warm oven. Turn the slow cooker to high and pour in flour and broth mixture and stir well. Cover and let cook about 10 minutes or until thickened. Pour over chops and some accompanying mashed potatoes.

Brown Sugar and Maple Glazed Ham

The glaze on this ham is absolutely sweet and delicious. You can add a few pineapple slices on top too if you wish, but you don't need them. Use only real maple syrup for this recipe. The manufactured stuff in the plastic bottles just doesn't do it justice.

Ingredients
1 – 5 to 6 pound fully cooked boneless ham
1/2 cup prepared Honey Dijon mustard
1/2 cup maple syrup
1/2 cup brown sugar, packed tight

Directions:
1. Spray a slow cooker with nonstick spray.
2. Make diamond cuts in the top of the ham and place it in the slow cooker.
3. In a large measuring cup, mix the mustard, syrup and the brown sugar. Mix with a whisk until it is blended well. It will be thick. Pour over the ham and spread around so that it covers the entire ham.
4. Place the lid on the slow cooker and cook on low 3 to 4 hours. Check with a meat thermometer to read 140 degrees F. Once it reaches this internal temperature, turn the slow cooker off.
5. Remove the ham from the slow cooker and cover loosely with foil. Let stand about 15 minutes.
6. In the meantime, strain the cooking juices and reserve in a gravy boat or measuring cup.
7. Slice the ham and pour the juices over top.

Crock Pot Pulled Pork

Many people complain that pulled pork is hard to make, but not with this recipe. It takes about 15 minutes of prep time and you are done until everything is cooked in about 8 hours or so. You use ginger ale in the recipe and it gives it a nice flavor. You can add some of your favorite barbecue sauce after everything is done cooking, or just leave the pulled pork without it. Either way, it is very good. Make sandwiches and serve with coleslaw.

Ingredients:
1 tablespoons light brown sugar
2 teaspoons paprika
1 teaspoon dry mustard
1/2 teaspoon cumin
1/4 teaspoon salt
1/4 teaspoon pepper
1 – 4 pound boneless pork shoulder, fat trimmed
2 teaspoons olive oil
3/4 cup water
1/2 cup apple cider vinegar
3 tablespoons tomato paste
2 more tablespoons brown sugar
1 can ginger ale plus enough water to make 2 cups
barbecue sauce

Directions:
1. Mix the 1 tablespoon brown sugar, paprika, mustard, cumin salt and pepper in a small bowl. Rub it all over the pork shoulder.
2. Heat a skillet to medium high and add the olive oil. Put the pork shoulder in and turn it to brown on all sides. Remove the pork from the skillet to a plate and whisk the 3/4 cup water into the drippings. Stir well and pour into a nonstick sprayed crock pot.

3. Add the vinegar, tomato paste and 2 more tablespoons of brown sugar to the crock pot and mix well. Carefully measure the ginger ale into a measuring cup and add enough water, if necessary, to make 2 cups. You will have to wait until the froth dies down to add the water. Pour into the crock pot.
4. Place the pork in the crock pot, cover and cook on low 8 hours. Do not cook on high. The flavors need to mingle for a whole 8 hours.
5. Remove the pork to a cutting board and set aside.
6. Strain the liquid into a saucepan and bring to a boil. Cook until the liquid is reduced by half. That should take about 10 minutes after boiling.
7. Pull the pork apart with two forks. It shouldn't be too hard as the slow cooking will make it extremely tender.
8. Place the pork in a large serving boil with 1 cup of the liquid in the sauce pan.
9. Do not mix in the barbecue sauce. Instead, let everyone add like ketchup on their bun.

Chapter 3: Top 10 Best Seafood Recipes

Seafood does very well in a crock pot. Fish, shellfish, shrimp, clams and more can be put into a slow cooker and cooked all day. Make shrimp scampi, gumbo, fish tacos, poached salmon, and yes, even tuna noodle hot dish in a crock pot. The nice part about doing seafood in the crock pot is that that scent of fish is not so prevalent Instead, you get the scent of the cooked dish and once you wash out the crock pot, it is gone.

Shrimp and Rice
When you purchase the shrimp, get the frozen kind that is already deveined, pre-cooked, peeled and does not have the tail on anymore. It might be more expensive, but it is so worth it not having to peel, devein and remove the tail.

Ingredients:
1 peeled and chopped yellow onion
2 to 3 cloves of garlic that have been finely chopped
1 chopped red bell pepper
1 chopped green bell pepper
1 cup chicken broth
1 can cream of chicken soup
1 can cream of celery soup
1 can Ro-tel
2 cups uncooked instant rice (do not use anything but the instant type)
1 teaspoon dried parsley
1 – 1/2 pounds shrimp

Directions:
1. Place the onion, garlic and peppers in a nonstick sprayed crock pot.
2. In a large measuring cup or bowl whisk together the chicken broth, cream of chicken and cream of celery soup until combined with no lumps. Pour over top of the vegetables.
3. Add the can of Ro-tel, rice and dried parsley in the crock pot
4. Dump in the frozen shrimp.
5. Cook on low for 6 to 8 hours and serve

Shrimp and Sausage Louisiana Gumbo
This deep south recipe adapted for the slow cooker gives you a real taste of the south with Creole flavors. It works well as a dinner or for a party, especially a Mardi Gras Party where you should probably double the recipe. Use the same type of shrimp used in the above recipe. This takes a little more attention and time because you have to cook some of the ingredients outside of the crock pot and you will need a cast iron frying pan to get the real deep south flavor.

Ingredients:
1/2 cup flour
1 pound Andouille sausage sliced in coins

4 peeled and chopped cloves of garlic
1 – 14.5 can of diced tomatoes
1 peeled and chopped yellow onion
1 chopped green bell pepper
2 ribs of celery that have been chopped
3 bay leaves
2 teaspoons Creole seasoning mix
1/2 teaspoon thyme
4 cups chicken broth
3 pounds shrimp-and-sausage
Green onions for garnish
Italian Flat Leaf Parsley for garnish

Directions:
1. Preheat your oven to 400 degrees F. Sprinkle the flour in a cast iron skillet and place in the preheated oven for about 5 minutes, stir, replace in the oven for 5 to 10 more minutes or until it gets brown. Remove from oven and let cool 10 minutes before proceeding.
2. Place sausage and garlic in a Dutch oven over medium heat and stir every once in a while for 5 minutes until it becomes brown. Remove and drain on paper towels. Place the sausage in a non-stick sprayed crock pot.
3. Add tomatoes, vegetables, bay leaves, Creole seasoning and thyme to the crock pot.
4. In the cast iron skillet, whisk the flour with the chicken broth until it becomes smooth. Pour into the slow cooker.
5. Cover and cook on High for about 6 hours.
6. Add shrimp, cover and cook on high for 30 more minutes stirring once or twice. Remove the bay leaves before serving and garnish with chopped green onion and flat leaf parsley.

Slow Cooker Shrimp Scampi
This is the easiest shrimp dish you will ever make. You kind of just dump everything in, turn the slow cooker on and eat some great deliciousness when it is done. The lemon and butter flavor is beyond compare. Use raw peeled and deveined shrimp for this recipe. If you put in frozen shrimp, it will make too much liquid.

Ingredients:
1/2 cup white wine (or just add a 1/2 cup more chicken broth)
1/4 cup chicken broth
2 tablespoons butter
2 tablespoons olive oil
2 tablespoons fresh minced flat leaf Italian parsley
1 tablespoon minced garlic
1 tablespoon lemon juice (use real juice from a lemon)
1/2 teaspoon salt

1/4 teaspoon pepper
1 pound shrimp
grated Parmesan cheese for garnish

Directions:
1. Pour the wine and chicken broth in the crock pot that has been sprayed with non-stick spray. Add the butter, olive oil, parsley, garlic, lemon juice, salt and pepper. Stir to combine.
2. Add the shrimp and cover. Cook 1-1/2 hours on high or 2-1/2 hours on low.
3. Serve with grated cheese on top

Slow Cooker Creamy Salmon Hot Dish
This recipe uses cans of salmon and creamy soups to achieve a casserole type dish that is delicious. Take this to a pot luck party and fish lovers will be asking for the recipe. Warning – This does tend to stick to the crock pot even if you spray it with nonstick spray. You might have to soak it for a couple hours to get everything clean again. Use a crock pot liner to make clean up a little easier.

Ingredients:
4 cups bread crumbs (use about 10 slices of soft bread ground in a food processor)
3 – 1 pound cans of salmon drained
1 – 16 ounce can tomato puree
1 chopped green pepper
6 beaten eggs
3 teaspoons fresh squeezed lemon juice
1 can cream of onion soup
2 chicken bouillon cubes that have been crushed
1 can cream of celery soup
1/2 cup milk

Directions:
1. Place liner in crock pot and spray with nonstick spray.
2. Place the bread crumbs in the bottom topped with the salmon. Add the tomato puree, green pepper, eggs, lemon juice, onion soup and bouillon cubes.
3. Cover and cook on low for 4 to 6 hours and high for about 3 to 4.
4. In a saucepan whisk the celery soup with the milk and heat over medium heat until it starts to bubble. Place in a gravy boat.
5. Scoop out servings into a bowl and top with the celery soup milk mixture.

Poached Salmon
This recipe is very good for dinner guests. They will think you slaved over the stove for hours when you really just dumped everything in a crock pot for a few hours. This does not take long to cook so you can put it on about 1 or 2 hours before guests arrive

Ingredients:
1 cup dry white wine
2 cups water
1 thin sliced lemon
1 thin sliced shallot
1 bay leaf
1 fresh tarragon sprig
2 sprigs fresh Italian parsley
2 sprigs dill
1 teaspoon black peppercorns, uncracked
1 teaspoon kosher salt
4 to 6 salmon fillets with the skin on
Olive oil
More kosher salt
Lemon wedges

Directions:
1. Pour the water, wine, lemon, shallots, bay leaf and herb sprigs into the crock pot. Add the salt and pepper.
2. Cook on high 30 minutes
3. Sprinkle the top of the salmon with salt and pepper. Put it in the crock pot skin side down.
4. Cover and cook on low until the salmon becomes opaque and flakes with a fork. Start checking after 45 minutes or an hour. If you don't want to serve right away, you can leave the crock pot on warm for up to 2 hours.
5. To serve, place the salmon on a serving plate and drizzle with olive oil and sprinkle with salt. Serve the salt wedges on the side.

Crock Pot Tuna Noodle Casserole
That old favorite can be made in a crock pot, which got many students that did not have a stove in their dorm room through a lot of long study nights. This recipe is slightly elevated by using dry sherry, but instead, you can just use 1 cup of milk instead or 1/3 cup chicken broth if you don't want to use alcohol. Most student dorms ban alcohol anyway. The noodles do have to be cooked first, but that can be done on a hot plate or in the microwave. You want them to be a little al dente and not soggy.

Ingredients:
10 ounces egg noodles, cooked and drained
1/3 cup sherry
2/3 cup milk
2 cans cream of celery or cream of mushroom soup
2 tablespoons dried parsley
2 cans tuna that have been drained well
2 tablespoons butter
10 ounces frozen peas

Directions:
1. Cook the egg noodles until still firm, drain and set aside until cool.
2. Combine the sherry, milk, cream of celery soup, parsley and tuna in a large bowl and mix well.
3. Pour the contents of the bowl into a nonstick sprayed crock pot. Dot with the butter
4. Cover and cook on low 6 hours. Add the frozen peas and cook on high 1 hour. Serve hot.

Fish Tacos

This recipe calls for tilapia, but you can use any white fish like haddock or cod. Fish tacos are a family favorite and there is hardly anything to do but put everything in the crock pot and let it cook. Place the fish in frozen and it is done in about 4 hours.

Ingredients:
6 frozen tilapia fillets
1 large can of Ro-tel, drained
1/4 cup fresh chopped cilantro
1/2 teaspoon minced garlic
2 tablespoons fresh lime juice
1/2 teaspoon salt1/4 teaspoon pepper
Soft Taco Shells, or hard if you prefer
Lettuce
Diced tomatoes
Salsa
Sour Cream

Directions:
1. Place the frozen fish in the bottom of a nonstick sprayed crock pot.
2. Cover over with Ro-tel, cilantro, garlic, lime juice, salt and pepper.
3. Cook on low for just 4 hours. Use a fork to flake the fish and mix with the rest of the ingredients in the crock pot.
4. Spoon into taco shells and top with shredded lettuce, diced tomatoes, salsa and sour cream.

Crab Legs in a Crock Pot

Steaming crab legs in the crock pot is a very easy way to make them and the meat is perfect every time. You can make this for the family or put the crock pot right on the buffet during a party. There won't be any left and you might need to make many more than what is in this recipe. Do not try to make this with a regular round crock pot. The oval one is needed merely to fit the legs in.

Ingredients:
3 pounds of Crab Legs
Water

1/2 stick of unsalted butter
4 peeled and minced garlic cloves
1 teaspoon dried dill weed.
Lemon and more melted butter for garnish

Directions:
1. Place rinsed crab legs in the crock pot
2. Pour in enough water to cover the crab legs
3. In a glass measuring cup, melt the butter and mix in the garlic and dill.
4. Pour the melted butter mixture over the crab legs in the pot
5. Cover and cook on high for 4 hours. (if the crab legs are frozen add another 30 minutes to the cook time)
6. Serve with melted butter and lemon

Clams with Tomato and Bacon
Clams cook up well in a slow cooker. The flavor is much better when they are slow simmered for a very long time under low heat. When you are ready to eat, just turn the heat up to high for another hour or so and you have a great seafood dish.

Ingredients:
6 thick cut slices of bacon
1/2 peeled and diced yellow onion
1 large can diced tomatoes
1 – 8 ounce bottle clam juice
1 teaspoon dried oregano
3 tablespoon capers with the juice
2 dozen littleneck clams that have been thoroughly cleaned.

Directions:
1. Cut the bacon in 1 inch pieces and fry in a skillet. Drain on paper towels
2. Cook the diced onion in the bacon drippings for about 1 minute
3. Put bacon and onions in a nonstick sprayed slow cooker. Add the tomatoes, clam juice, oregano and caper and stir.
4. Cover and cook on low for 3 to 4 hours.
5. About 1 hour before you want to serve, turn up the heat on the crock pot to high. Wait 15 minutes and put the clams in. Cover and cook for 30 to 40 minutes. DO NOT LIFT THE LID. Look through the glass to make sure the clams are opening. Those that do not open, need to be discarded.
6. Serve with some linguine and sauce

Seafood Feast
This recipe includes all kinds of seafood. There are shrimp – get the peeled and deveined variety, scallops and crabs in this dish all in a buttery and creamy sauce which can be served over cooked rice or egg noodles. This feast is a delicious meal on a cool fall evening even if you live miles away from an ocean.

Ingredients:
1 pound bay scallops
1 pound peeled and deveined shrimp
1 pound crab meat
2 cans of cream of celery soup
milk – fill the 2 soup cans with milk to measure
2 tablespoons unsalted butter that has been softened
1 teaspoon Old Bay Seasoning
1/4 teaspoon salt
1/4 teaspoon pepper

Directions:
1. Spray the crock pot with nonstick spray and layer in the scallops, crab meat and shrimp
2. In a large bowl whisk together the soup and milk until it is smooth and well combined. Pour it over the seafood in the crock pot.
3. Place the butter in a bowl and mix in the seasonings with a fork until well combined. Pour this over the top
4. Cover and cook on low for 3 to 4 hours.
5. Serve with rice or noodles.

Chapter 4: Top 10 Best Soup and Stew Recipes

Soup and stew are a staple dinner or lunch in most households. Soups and stews utilize just a little bit of meat, lots of vegetables, beans, rice and other fillers and give you a hardy meal for just cents on the dollar. Every home should have an arsenal of soup and stew recipes ready for those lean times when there might not be much money to spend on food. The following soups and stews are some common favorites and some that are a little different. All of them cook up wonderfully in the slow cooker and provide the family a delicious meal alongside some crusty bread.

Chicken Noodle Soup in a Crock Pot
Cooking Chicken noodle soup in a crock pot is just a little bit easier than in a stock pot on the stove. You don't have to worry about anything burning and it still cooks up rich and lovely. The kids will love it. Make it when someone in the house has a cold. The old wives tale of chicken noodle soup helping a cold is true. The heat from the soup makes the sinuses open so you can breathe.

Ingredients:
1 small peeled and chopped onion
2 peeled and chopped carrots
3 stalks chopped celery
3 pounds chicken pieces
4 cups water
4 cups chicken broth
salt and pepper to taste
1 tablespoon minced garlic
1/4 cup fresh chopped parsley
1 bay leaf
1/2 teaspoon dried marjoram
6 ounces medium egg noodles

Directions:
1. Peel and chop all the vegetables and put them in the bottom of a non-stick sprayed crock pot. Add the chicken pieces and pour in the water and broth. Add salt and pepper to taste, garlic, parsley, bay leaf and marjoram.
2. Cover and cook on low for 5 to 6 hours
3. Remove the chicken and bay leaf from the pot. Remove the meat from the bone and dice, placing the diced chicken back in the crock pot.
4. Add the noodles
5. Put the cover back on and cook for 45 minutes to 1 hour on low or turn to high and cook 20 to 30 more minutes or until the noodles are tender and not hard or mushy.
6. Serve with crusty bread

Crock Pot Cream of Potato Soup

This soup is super creamy and the flavors of onion, potato and bacon are simply wonderful on a cold night. This soup will stick to your ribs. You can add 1 to 2 cups shredded cheddar to it at the end before serving to make it cheesy too. Garnish it with some chopped green onion and chives just before serving.

Ingredients:
1 teaspoon olive oil
2 teaspoons minced garlic
1 sweet or yellow onion that has been peeled and finely chopped
6 slices of bacon
2 (10.5 ounce) cans of chicken broth
2 cups water
1/2 teaspoon salt
1/2 teaspoon cracked pepper
1 tablespoon dried parsley
5 to 6 potatoes that have been peeled and diced
1/2 cup flour
2 cups half and half
1 – 12 fluid ounce can of evaporated milk

Directions:
1. Pour olive oil in a hot skillet over medium heat and add the garlic and onion. Sauté until the onion is translucent
2. Cut the bacon in 1/2 inch pieces and place in the frying pan. Cook until brown. Scoop out the bacon pieces, garlic and onion and drain on a paper towel.
3. Place the bacon, garlic and onion in the bottom of a nonstick sprayed crock pot.
4. Stir in the broth, water, salt, pepper and parsley.
5. Add the diced potatoes, cover and cook on low for 7 hours and stir every once in a while.
6. Right before the 7 hours is up, take the flour and half and half in a bowl and whisk it together. Stir it into the crock pot and add the evaporated milk. Cover and cook 30 minutes on high. Garnish with green onion and chives and serve.

Homemade Beef and Barley Soup in a Slow Cooker
It only takes about 10 minutes to sauté the beef, chop the vegetables and put this meal together. You can even do that the night before, dump everything in the slow cooker in the morning and be out the door early. When you come home, the soup will be ready and you just have to cut up some nice crusty bread to eat with it.

Ingredients:
2 tablespoons olive oil
1 tablespoon minced garlic
1 small peeled and chopped yellow onion

4 stalks of celery that have been chopped
6 large carrots peeled and chopped
1 tablespoon more of olive oil
1-1/2 pounds lean beef that has been cubed
1/2 teaspoon salt
1/2 teaspoon pepper
3 – 10.5 ounce cans of beef broth
6 cups water
1 cup barley
1 teaspoon dried thyme

Directions:
1. Pour the 2 tablespoons olive oil in a skillet warmed over medium high heat. Add the garlic, onion, celery and carrots and sauté for about 3 to 4 minutes or until onions become translucent
2. Remove to a nonstick sprayed slow cooker.
3. Pour the one tablespoon olive oil back into the skillet and add the beef. Season with the salt and pepper and brown on all sides, for about 4 to 5 minutes and place on top of the vegetables in the slow cooker.
4. Add a little bit of the beef broth to the skillet to get all the brown bits out and pour into the slow cooker with the rest of the beef broth and water.
5. Add the barley, cover and cook for 6 to 8 hours on low.
6. Add the thyme 15 minutes before serving.

Crock pot Broccoli and Three Cheese Soup
Broccoli Cheese Soup is thick and rich and almost everyone loves it. This recipe uses three different kinds of cheese. The first is processed cheese, like Velveeta and there is also Parmesan and Cheddar. These cheeses give the soup a little more flavor and zip. Serve with a salad and big crusty croutons for a delicious dinner on a cold night.

Ingredients:
1/4 cup butter
1 large peeled and chopped yellow onion
1 tablespoon minced garlic
1/4 cup flour
1 – 12 ounce can evaporated milk
4 cups chicken broth
1/2 teaspoon salt
1/2 teaspoon pepper
1 – 14 ounce bag of frozen baby broccoli florets that has been thawed
1 – 8 ounce loaf of processed cheese product (Velveeta)
1 -1/2 cups shredded Cheddar
1 cup shredded Parmesan cheese

Directions:

1. Melt butter in a skillet over medium high heat
2. Sauté the onion and garlic for about 4 minutes or until onion is tender
3. Add the flour and stir well cooking for about 1 minute stirring constantly. Pour the evaporated milk in slowly and whisk until the mixture is very smooth.
4. Pour the mixture into a nonstick sprayed crock pot
5. Stir in the broth, salt, pepper and broccoli. Cover and cook on low for 4 hours. The mixture should start to bubble.
6. Cut the processed cheese loaf into cubes and place in the crock pot with the Cheddar and Parmesan. Stir until everything melts and the soup is ready to serve. You can garnish with a little more grated Parmesan on top of each bowl before serving.

French Onion Soup Crock pot Style
French Onion Soup is a very elegant dinner soup to serve as an appetizer. It is tasty and cheesy and has a bit of bread floating on the surface. The onions are normally caramelized in a sauté pan, but when making this soup in a crock pot, you don't have to worry about that since everything happens naturally over the long cook time.

Ingredients:
1/4 cup unsalted butter
1 bay leaf
1 teaspoon dried thyme
5 pounds large sweet onions that have been peeled and sliced vertically (16 cups)
1 tablespoon sugar
2 tablespoons red wine vinegar
6 cups low salt beef stock
1 teaspoon Kosher salt
1 teaspoon pepper
24 slices of French Bread (a baguette works well)
5 ounces or about 1 -14 cups shredded Gruyere cheese

Directions:
1. Spray the crock pot with nonstick spray and place the butter, cut in small slices in the bottom of the crock pot. Add the bay leaf and thyme.
2. Add onions and sprinkle with the sugar. Cook on High for 8 hours to caramelize the onions.
3. Remove the bay leaf and discard it. Add the vinegar, stock, salt, and pepper and cook covered on High for 30 more minutes.
4. Preheat the broiler of you oven to high.
5. Cover two baking sheets with foil and place the bread in a single layer on them and broil for 30 seconds on both sides or until they are toasty brown.
6. Ladle about 1 cup of the soup in 12 – oven proof ramekins. Top with 2 slices of bread and 2 tablespoons of the cheese or more.

7. Put the ramekins on a jelly-roll pan and slid into the oven again broiling for 2 minutes until the cheese melts and starts to get brown. Serve immediately.

Easy Crock Pot Beef Stew
This is a very hardy stew and you will never go back to making stew in a pot on the oven. The meat gets very tender in the crock pot when cooking for long times over low heat. It will literally melt in your mouth.

Ingredients:
1 tablespoon olive oil
1 clove of garlic that has been minced
1 peeled and chopped yellow or sweet onion
4 large carrots peeled and sliced
2 stalks celery that have been chopped
1 more tablespoon olive oil
2 pounds stew beef cut in cubes
1/4 cup flour
1/2 teaspoon salt
1/2 teaspoon pepper
1 bay leaf
1 teaspoon paprika
1 teaspoon Worcestershire sauce
1-1/2 cups beef broth
3 large potatoes that have been peeled and diced

Directions:
1. Heat 1 tablespoon olive oil over medium heat in a large skillet. Sauté the garlic, onion, carrots and celery for about 4 minutes or until tender. Put in the bottom of a nonstick sprayed crock pot.
2. Put the other tablespoon olive oil in the skillet and brown the meat that has been tossed with flour, salt and pepper. Just lightly brown on all sides and put into the crock pot.
3. Place in the crock pot, the bay leaf, paprika, Worcestershire sauce, beef broth and potatoes and give the pot a stir.
4. Cover and cook on low 10 to 12 hours or on high for 4 to 6 hours. The stew should thicken up all by itself. The only thing you have to do before serving is take out the bay leaf.

Incredible Chicken Stew
This savory stew will quickly become a family favorite. You use leg quarters, but if the family does not like dark meat, you can substitute with 3 large chicken breast halves. You can even shred the meat after it cooks and put it back in the crock pot. It doesn't take much to shred it because the chicken is so tender when it is done. Put what needs to go in the crock pot on high for 1 hour in before you get ready for work in the morning, add the rest of the ingredients, turn the heat

down and go to work. You can add a can of canaloni beans to the stew instead of potatoes if desired.

Ingredients:
1 can (10-3/4 ounces) cream of mushroom soup (can use cream of chicken)
1/3 cup water
1 teaspoon salt
1/2 teaspoon pepper
1/2 teaspoon garlic powder
4 chicken leg quarter with skin removed, the thigh removed from the leg
3 medium potatoes that have been peeled and cubed
2 medium peeled and chopped yellow onions
1 cup frozen corn that has been thawed and drained
1 – 8 ounce can tomato sauce
1 envelope onion soup mix

Directions:
1. Place the can of cream of mushroom soup and water in a nonstick sprayed crock pot and whisk together until smooth. Add the salt, pepper and garlic powder.
2. Place the chicken and cover and cook on high for 1 hour.
3. Put in the potatoes, onions, corn, tomato sauce and onion soup mix and cover and cook for 6 to 8 hours on low or 4 hours on high.
4. Remove the chicken from the crock pot with a slotted spoon and shred or chop removing the bones. Put it back in the crock pot, stir and serve.

Crock Pot Irish Lamb Stew
Those that like lamb will love this stew. You use a boneless leg of lamb, leeks, potatoes and carrots to make a very hardy stew that tastes divine. Serve with crusty bread and a salad to finish the meal. Leeks are a little hard to work with. You have to use only the white part and you have to separate each leaf and wash because dirt can get encrusted on the leek. You don't want any of the dirt in your stew, so wash well before adding to the crock pot. Leeks give a different flavor that is a cross between a regular onion and green onion.

Ingredients:
3 large leeks, white part only
1-1/2 pounds of peeled potatoes cut in 1 inch pieces
3 large peeled carrots cut in 1 inch pieces
3 stalks celery that has been sliced thin
1 -14 ounce can chicken broth
2 teaspoon fresh chopped thyme
1 teaspoon salt
1 teaspoon pepper
1/4 cup fresh chopped parsley
2 pounds boneless leg of lamb that has been trimmed and cut in 1 inch pieces

Directions:
1. Remove green part of leek and discard. Separate all the leaves of the whit part and wash well. Place in the crock pot that has been sprayed with nonstick spray
2. Add the potatoes, carrots and celery.
3. Add the chicken broth, chopped thyme, salt and pepper
4. Cover and cook on low for 8 hours.
5. Right before serving, stir in the fresh parsley and let cook 15 more minutes on high.

Slow Cooker Cider and Pork Stew

Serve this lovely stew in the fall when the apples are ripening. You can have it any time, but at that time of the year, it seems to just taste better. Take your pork shoulder and trim the fat and cut the meat into 3/4 inch cubes or cut it into 1/2 inch sections, cook and remove to shred the pork. Put the shredded pork back in the crock pot and serve.

Ingredients:
3 tablespoons flour
1 teaspoon salt
1 teaspoon pepper
1/4 teaspoon dried thyme
2 pounds boneless pork shoulder
6 carrots that have been peeled and cut into coins
4 medium potatoes that have been peeled and cut into cubes
1 cup peeled and chopped yellow onion
2 cups apple cider
1 tablespoon vinegar
1/2 cup cold water
1/4 cup more of flour

Directions:
1. Whisk together the 3 tablespoons flour, salt, pepper and thyme. Toss the cubes of meat or rub the sections of meat with it.
2. Place the carrots, potatoes and onion in the nonstick sprayed crock pot and top with the floured meat.
3. In a large glass measuring cup, combine the apple cider and the vinegar. Slowly pour over the meat. Cover and cook on low for 9 to 11 hours
4. Turn the crock pot to high. Place the cold water and 1/4 cup flour in a container and stir it until it is smooth. Stir this into the crock pot and cook on low for 15 more minutes to thicken the stew.

Kielbasa Stew in a Slow Cooker

This stew is chock full of good things including white beans, tomatoes and baby spinach. It is a little different, but very good. Serve with bread or a salad to make a delicious, protein filled dinner.

Ingredients;
14 ounces of kielbasa, sliced in 1/2 inch coins
1 pound dried white beans (Navy beans work well)
4 cups low salt chicken broth
1 – 14.5 ounce can of diced tomatoes
1 large peeled and chopped onion
1 teaspoon dried rosemary
1 cup water
6 cups baby spinach

Directions:
1. Slice the Kielbasa and put in the bottom of a nonstick sprayed slow cooker.
2. Pour in the dried beans, broth, tomatoes with juice, onion and rosemary and pour water over top.
3. Cover and cook on low 7 to 8 hours or on high for 6 hours. The beans should be tender when done.
4. Turn the slow cooker on high and add the spinach right before serving and let cook 15 more minutes and serve.

Chapter 5: Top 10 Best Vegetarian Recipes

The following are some non-meat recipes for those that like to eat vegetarian or have vegetarian friends. It is good for everyone to eat a meatless meal once in in a while and these are very delicious. You won't miss the meat even in the recipes that are supposed to look like there is meat in them. There are recipes for chili, Southwestern and Latin American inspired dishes, a curry dish and recipes that will make you not miss having meat in a meal.

Chili with White Beans and Some Crunch

The crunch in this recipe comes from corn chips. Some of the onions and bell peppers are processed into a sauce and the rest are put in the crock pot as they are. When the recipe says divided, watch in the directions for how much you put where. This dish will have your family coming back again and again. The white beans gives the recipe a great deal of protein and good fiber so that you will fill up without any meat.

Ingredients:
3 cups peeled and chopped onions, divided
3 cups chopped red bell pepper, divided (you can use any color bell pepper)
1 tablespoon dry oregano
1/2 cup fresh chopped cilantro
3 garlic cloves
3 dried ancho chilies
1/4 cup olive oil
1/2 tablespoon ground cumin
2 tablespoons tomato paste
1/2 teaspoon coriander
1 teaspoon kosher salt
1 teaspoon pepper
1 bay leaf
4 – 1/2 cups vegetarian vegetable stock
1 – 26 ounce tomato puree
1 – 16 ounce package of dried white beans
4 cups zucchini that has been peeled and diced
1 – 15 ounce can diced tomatoes
sour cream
corn chips

Directions:
1. Place 1 cup of the onion, 1 cup of the bell pepper, the oregano, cilantro and peeled garlic cloves in a food processor. Remove the seeds and stems from the ancho chilies and chop. Add to the food processor and process until the mixture is almost smooth.
2. Pour the oil into a large skillet. Heat over medium and pour the mixture in the food processor in. Cook for about 8 minutes or until the mixture starts

to evaporate. Stir it constantly. Add the cumin, tomato paste, coriander, salt, pepper and bay leaf and cook, while stirring, about 2 more minutes.
3. Place the mixture in the skillet into a nonstick sprayed crock pot. Add the rest of the onions and 1 more cup of the bell pepper (there should be one more cup left). Add the stock, puree, beans and stir. Place the cover on and cook on low for 8 hours.
4. Change the temperature to high on the crock pot and add the remaining cup of bell peppers, zucchini, and diced tomatoes. Cook on high for 20 minutes.
5. When ready to serve, remove bay leaf, ladle into bowls and top with a dollop of sour cream and a handful of crushed corn chips.

Vegetarian Chili and Sweet Potatoes
I don't know exactly where this recipe hails from but it has some unusual ingredients including cocoa powder and cinnamon. It reminds me of a South African sweet potato stew recipe I once tried. You would not think cocoa and cinnamon would taste good with sweet potatoes, tomatoes and beans, but it sure does. The recipe calls for a can of diced tomatoes. If you can find fire-roasted diced tomatoes, it adds a little extra flavor to the dish.

Ingredients:
4 peeled and chopped garlic cloves
1 peeled and chopped red onion
1 chopped green bell pepper
1/4 teaspoon ground cinnamon
2 teaspoons unsweetened cocoa powder
1 tablespoon chili powder
1 tablespoon cumin
1 teaspoon kosher salt
1/2 teaspoon ground black pepper
1 -28 ounce can of diced tomatoes
1 – 15 ounce can of black beans that have been drained and rinsed
1 – 15 ounce can of light kidney beans, drained and rinsed
1 large sweet potato that has been peeled and diced
1 cup water
Sour Cream
Green Onions
Tortilla Chips

Directions:
1. Spray a crock pot with nonstick spray. Add the garlic, onion, bell pepper, cinnamon, cocoa powder, chili powder, cumin, salt and pepper and mix well.
2. Add the tomatoes (do not drain) and drained and rinsed beans. Also add the diced sweet potato and water.
3. Cover and cook on low for 7 to 8 hours or on high for 4 to 5 hours or until the sweet potato is tender.

4. Ladle into a bowl and serve with sour cream and thin sliced green onion on top and sprinkle with crushed tortilla chips.

Crock Pot Sloppy Joes Vegetarian Style
No, this recipe does not contain ground beef. Instead it is made with protein and fiber rich pinto beans. The flavor and texture is very much like a regular sloppy Joe and it is guaranteed that the kids will like it because of the spicy flavor.

Ingredients:
1 -1/2 tablespoon olive oil
2 cloves peeled and minced garlic
1 large white onion that has been peeled and sliced thin
2 medium sized carrots that have been peeled and sliced thin
2 tablespoons Balsamic vinegar
2 tablespoons chili powder
1 cup dry pinto beans that have been soaked in enough water to cover, overnight
1 large chopped red bell pepper
1 – 8 ounce can tomato sauce
1/2 cup water
2 tablespoons tomato paste
2 tablespoons soy sauce
4 cups cabbage that has been thinly sliced
1 zucchini that has been chopped
1 cup frozen corn kernels
2 tablespoons honey mustard
1 teaspoon salt
1 tablespoon brown sugar
1 teaspoon salt
8 to 10 hamburger buns (whole wheat preferred)

Directions:
1. Place the olive oil in a heated skillet over medium heat and add the garlic, onion and carrot. Sauté until the onion is tender, about 3 to 6 minutes. Remove from heat and add the vinegar stirring all the brown bits up from the pan. Stir in the chili powder
2. Spray the crock pot with nonstick spray. Drain and rinse the beans and place them in the crock pot. Add the bell pepper, tomato sauce, water and paste stirring well.
3. Spread the onion carrot mixture on top. This will keep the beans in liquid while cooking so they become tender and do not dry. Cover and cook on for 5 hours and low for 9 hours.
4. Add the cabbage, zucchini and thawed and drained corn kernels Stir in the honey mustard brown sugar and salt and cook on high for about 30 minutes.
5. When ready to serve, spread the mixture on buns.

Cheesy Bean and Rice Casserole in the Slow Cooker

This dish is super easy to make and everyone will want more. It uses black eyed peas but you can use just about any type of bean instead. Cook your rice ahead of time and let it cool so that it keeps its integrity in the slow cooker and soak the beans overnight to help them soften up. This recipe does have a distinct Southwestern flavor and is spicy Reduce the spices if you want it to be a little more tame.

Ingredients:
1 – 1/2 cups dried black-eyed peas
1 diced red bell pepper
1 medium peeled and diced yellow onion
2 cloves of chopped garlic
1 – 28 ounce can of diced tomatoes with juices
1 – 10 ounce can corn that has been drained
1/4 cup chili powder
2 teaspoons cumin
2 cups rice that has been cooked and cooled
1/2 to 1 cup shredded Cheddar

Directions:
1. Drain and rinse the black-eyed peas and put in the bottom of a nonstick sprayed slow cooker. Add the bell pepper, onion, garlic, tomatoes and juices and corn . Stir well.
2. Cook on high for only 2 hours.
3. Stir in the chili powder and cumin, rice and cheese and cook for 30 more minutes. The mixture should be thick and rich.

Note: Take the chili powder down to 2 tablespoons and cumin to 1/2 teaspoon for a "not-so-spicy" version and serve with sour cream.

Couscous with Vegetable Curry
If you like curry, you will love the flavor of this dish. It is very spicy and will clear your sinuses, but leave you with a very pleasant aftertaste. It uses yogurt instead of sour cream to lend a cooling effect.

Ingredients:
4 cups peeled and diced Russet potatoes
4 cups fresh chopped tomato
1 cup peeled and chopped yellow onion
1 cup peeled and chopped carrot
1 teaspoon salt
1/4 teaspoon cayenne pepper
2 tablespoons curry powder
2 teaspoons cumin
2 – 15 ounce cans garbanzo beans that have been rinsed and drained
1 green bell pepper cut into strips
3 cloves peeled garlic minced
4 green onions, chopped

1/3 cup fresh chopped cilantro
3 cups hot cooked couscous
6 tablespoon raisins
6 tablespoons prepared mango chutney
6 tablespoons plain yogurt

Directions:
1. Put the peeled and diced potatoes in the bottom of a nonstick sprayed slow cooker.
2. Combine the tomato, onion, carrot, salt, cayenne, curry and cumin in a bowl and stir. Put this mixture over the potatoes
3. Cover and cook on low for 9 hours.
4. Stir in the green onion and cilantro and cook for an additional 10 minutes.
5. Place couscous in a bowl and ladle the crock pot mixture over top. Top each serving with raisins, chutney and yogurt.

One Layer at a Time Veggie Casserole
The trick to this dish is no trick at all. You just layer everything in the crock pot like a big lasagna. It comes out looking like lasagna too, but it is totally made from vegetables.

Ingredients:
1 – 14.5 ounce can of tomato sauce
1 tablespoon Italian Herbs
1/2 teaspoon salt
1/4 teaspoon pepper
4 peeled and thinly sliced potatoes
2 large peeled and thinly sliced zucchini
2 peeled and thinly sliced carrots
1/2 cup frozen corn, divided
1/2 cup frozen peas, divided
More salt and pepper to taste
1-1/2 cups shredded Cheddar

Directions:
1. Pour the tomato sauce in a large bowl and add the Italian Herbs, salt and pepper. Mix well and set aside.
2. Spray nonstick spray in a crock pot and layer the bottom with half the potatoes overlapping them slightly so they completely cover the bottom. Sprinkle with a little salt and pepper.
3. Layer half the zucchini over top and sprinkle with a little salt and pepper.
4. Put half the carrots in, distributing it evenly over the zucchini
5. Put in half the frozen corn and peas, distributing it evenly over the carrots.
6. Pour in half the sauce mixture.
7. Sprinkle with half of the cheese
8. Place another tight layer of potatoes over top followed by a sprinkle of salt and pepper and another layer of zucchini, carrots, corn and peas.

9. Add the rest of the sauce.
10. Sprinkle the top with the cheese.
11. Cook on high for 3 to 4 hours and serve.

Vegetable Stuffed Peppers
These peppers are stuffed with rice, beans, cheese and a lot of other good stuff. They cook up nice and tender in the crock pot and you will never miss the meat.

Ingredients:
3 small tomatoes that have been chopped
1 small peeled and chopped sweet onion
1 cup frozen corn kernels that has been thawed and drained
1/3 cup kidney beans that have been rinsed and drained
1/3 cup black beans that have been rinsed and drained
2 cups brown rice that has been cooked
3/4 cup Monterey Jack cheese that has been cubed
4 fresh basil leaves that have been thinly sliced
3 cloves of minced garlic
1/2 teaspoon salt
1/4 teaspoon pepper
3/4 cup meatless spaghetti sauce
1/2 cup water
6 large sweet peppers that have been hollowed out
4 tablespoons Parmesan cheese

Directions:
1. Combine the chopped tomatoes, chopped onion, corn, kidney beans, black beans brown rice, cheese, basil, garlic, salt and pepper in a big bowl and mix gently to combine.
2. Mix the sauce and water in a bowl and pour half in the bottom of a nonstick sprayed crock pot.
3. Fill the 6 peppers with the mixture and place in the crock pot.
4. Pour the rest of the sauce over top and sprinkle with just 2 tablespoons of the Parmesan.
5. Cover and cook on low for 3 to 4 hours or until the peppers are tender. Sprinkle with the rest of the Parmesan and serve.

Bean and Spinach Enchiladas in the Slow Cooker
Those that enjoy Mexican inspired dishes will love this slow cooker meal. You make a salad with vegetables and a lime and oil dressing to serve on the side. It is a little different, but very good and there is no meat involved. This recipe uses black beans, but you can use any kind of bean you prefer. I've made it with pintos, great northern, Navy beans and black beans and it tastes equally as delicious. In a family of four, you will each get 2 enchiladas, so if you are making this dish for more people, be sure to use a large oval slow cooker and double the recipe.

Ingredients:
1 regular can of black beans that has been rinsed and drained
1 cup frozen corn
1 – 10 ounce package of frozen chopped spinach
1/2 teaspoon cumin
1/4 teaspoon salt
1/4 teaspoon pepper
2 cups shredded sharp Cheddar cheese, divided
3 – 1/2 cups commercial or homemade salsa (2 jars commercial salsa)
8 – 6 inch corn tortillas made warm so they are pliable
6 cups chopped Romaine lettuce
4 radishes cut thin
1/2 cup cherry tomatoes halved
1/2 cucumber that has been peeled, halved and sliced thin
3 tablespoons fresh squeezed lime juice
2 tablespoons olive oil
pinch salt and pepper
Sour cream
Green Onions that have been sliced thin

Directions:
1. Drain and rinse beans. Thaw corn and spinach and drain. Get excess water out of spinach by squishing it with a form in a strainer or by putting it between paper towels and squeezing to get as much liquid out of it as possible.
2. Place half the beans in a bowl and mash with a fork. Add all the corn, spinach, cumin and half of the Cheddar. Add the rest of the beans and the salt and pepper. Mix well to combine. This is the filling for the tortillas
3. Spread half the salsa in the bottom of a nonstick sprayed slow cooker.
4. Place about 1/2 cup of the filling on each of the warmed tortilla shells and carefully roll. Place each enchilada with the seam side down in the salsa at the bottom of the slow cooker.
5. Top with the rest of the salsa and cheese, cover and cook on high for ONLY 3 hours.
6. Right before serving, place the chopped Romaine, radishes, tomatoes and cucumber in a bowl and toss. In a small bowl combine the lime juice and oil with a pinch of salt and pepper and whisk well. Pour over vegetables and serve alongside the enchiladas.
7. Place a dollop of sour cream on each enchilada and sprinkle with green onions.

Crock Pot Bolognese of Cauliflower
Bolognese is usually made with meat that gives it its chunky texture. Instead of meat, this recipe uses fresh cauliflower that is mashed after being cooked. It is absolutely delectable and you can serve it over whole wheat noodles or egg noodles.

Ingredients:
1 fresh head of cauliflower
1 cup peeled and diced red onion
2 cloves minced garlic
2 teaspoons dried oregano
1 teaspoon dried basil
2 – 14 ounce cans of fire-roasted diced tomatoes (regular tomatoes works fine too)
1/2 cup vegetable broth
1/4 teaspoon red pepper flakes
1/4 teaspoon salt
1/4 teaspoon pepper

Directions:
1. Prepare cauliflower by cutting the head into florets and placing them in the bottom of a nonstick sprayed slow cooker
2. Add the onion, garlic, dried herbs, tomatoes, vegetable broth, pepper flakes, salt and pepper.
3. Cover and cook on high for 5 hours.
4. Mash the cauliflower with a fork or potato masher before serving over noodles.

Slow Cooker Mushroom Stroganoff
If you like mushrooms, you will love this stroganoff recipe. Use any type of mushrooms or a variety of different types. I typically use some Portobello mushrooms because they are so meaty, but I mix in other smaller white mushrooms as well. Never use canned mushrooms in this recipe because they will become a slimy mess. Use fresh ones and prepare them by removing and trimming stems and/or gills as the variety dictates.

Ingredients:
5 cups prepared mushrooms
1 large onion that has been peeled and thinly sliced
2 cloves peeled and minced garlic
1 – 1/2 cup vegetable stock
3 teaspoons paprika
1/2 teaspoon salt
1/4 teaspoon pepper
1/2 cup sour cream
1/4 cup fresh chopped parsley

Directions:
1. Place mushrooms onion, garlic, stock, paprika, salt and pepper into a nonstick sprayed crock pot and stir to mix.
2. Cover and cook on high for 4 hours.

3. Stir in the sour cream, replace the cover and cook on high another 15 minutes.
4. Serve over noodles and sprinkle with fresh parsley.

Chapter 6: Top 10 Best Pasta and Grain Recipes

Did you know you can make pasta in the crock pot? It is very easy to make pasta and grain dishes and they are rarely over or under cooked. You can make anything from lasagna to macaroni and cheese, all the way to couscous and other grain dishes in the crock pot. Everything will stay steaming hot until you want to serve.

Slow Cooker Ravioli
This easy dish is made from frozen ravioli and jarred sauce, but you can also use homemade sauce. Use either cheese or beef filled ravioli that go in frozen and come out tender and delicious.

Ingredients;
1 tablespoon olive oil
1 medium peeled and chopped sweet onion
1 clove minced garlic
2 – 26 ounce jars of four cheese tomato pasta sauce
1 – 15 ounce can of tomato sauce
1-1/2 teaspoon dried Italian seasonings
1/4 teaspoon salt
2 – 25 ounce packages of frozen ravioli
2 cups shredded mozzarella cheese
1/4 cup fresh chopped flat leaf parsley

Directions:
1. Heat a large skillet over medium heat. Pour in the olive oil and sauté the onion and garlic for about 4 minutes or until the onion is tender.
2. Add the pasta and tomato sauce along with the Italian seasonings and stir.
3. Place 1 cup of the sauce mixture in the bottom of a nonstick sprayed slow cooker.
4. Add one of the packages of frozen ravioli and sprinkle 1 cup of the mozzarella cheese on top.
5. Layer the second bag of frozen ravioli on along with the rest of the cheese and pour all of the remaining sauce in the skillet over top.
6. Cover and cook on low for 5 to 6-1/2 hours.
7. Sprinkle with chopped parsley right before serving.

Crock Pot Lasagna
Lasagna is a favorite recipe in our household. This recipe uses dry lasagna noodles in the crock pot with other ingredients and it always comes out perfect. You do have to carefully break the dry noodles to fit into the curves of the pot and it is beneficial to use a large, oval size crock pot instead of a round one. This

recipe uses Swiss chard, but you can use baby spinach instead or eliminate it completely if you don't want any green vegetables in your lasagna.

Ingredients:
3 cloves of peeled and chopped garlic
2 – 28 ounce cans of diced tomatoes
1 – 16 ounce container Ricotta cheese
1/4 teaspoon salt
1/4 teaspoon pepper
1/2 cup chopped flat leaf parsley
1/2 cup grated Parmesan cheese
1 – 12 ounce package of dry lasagna noodles
1 bunch Swiss chard that has been torn into small pieces
1 – 12 ounce package of shredded mozzarella cheese

Directions:
1. Place the garlic and diced tomatoes in a bowl and stir together
2. Place the Ricotta, salt, pepper, parsley and Parmesan in another bowl and mix well.
3. Spray a crock pot with non-stick spray and put enough of the tomato mixture in the bottom to cover.
4. Put in a layer of dry lasagna noodles to fit the bottom.
5. Place a layer of Swiss chard on top and place about 1/3 of the Ricotta cheese mixture in dollops on top of the chard.
6. Spread another layer of tomato sauce and sprinkle with some mozzarella
7. Continue layering noodles, Swiss chard, Ricotta, tomato sauce and mozzarella until you have no more ingredients ending with the mozzarella
8. Cook on low for only 2 to 3 hours. The noodles should be tender.
9. Turn to warm and let set for about 15 to 20 minutes and serve.

Slow Cooker Spiral Pasta with Italian Sausage and Peppers
This brings a pasta twist (in spirals) to Italian Sausage and Peppers. The scent will start attracting attention in about an hour or so and it only takes about 3 to 4 hours to make. By the time you are ready to eat, everyone will be salivating. The recipe calls for 2 green and 1 red pepper, but you can use any combination including yellow and purple peppers if desired. It also uses a combination of sweet and hot sausage to give it just the right punch. If you don't like hot sausage, just use 2 pounds of the sweet sausage. I use bulk sausage but you can use links or small patties if you like and chop them up before serving.

Ingredients:
1 teaspoon olive oil
1 large sweet onion that has been peeled and sliced thin
1 clove peeled and minced garlic
1 pound sweet Italian sausage
1 pound hot Italian sausage
1 red bell pepper, seeded and sliced in strips

2 green bell peppers, seeded and sliced in strips
1 – 24 ounce jar of your favorite pasta sauce
salt and pepper to taste
1 – 16 ounce package of spiral pasta or macaroni

Directions:
1. Heat up a large skillet and add the olive oil. Sauté the onion and garlic until tender.
2. Add all the sausage and just brown. Drain excess grease.
3. Place the sausage mixture in the bottom of a nonstick sprayed crock pot and add the peppers and pasta sauce. Add salt and pepper to taste
4. Cook on high 3 to 4 hours.
5. Before cooking is done boil the pasta as per package directions until still firm. Drain. Serve the sausage and peppers over the pasta.

Crock Pot Stuffed Spinach and Ricotta Manicotti
Use frozen spinach, ricotta and variety of flavored pasta sauces to make this crock pot pasta meal. It is very easy to make and the family will love it just as much as the love your lasagna.

Ingredients:
1 – 15 ounce container ricotta cheese
1 – 10 ounce package of frozen spinach that has been thawed and squeezed dry as possible
1 slightly beaten egg
1/2 cup grated Parmesan cheese, divided
1/2 cup shredded mozzarella cheese
1/4 teaspoon salt
1/4 teaspoon pepper
1 – 24 ounce jar pasta sauce with roasted garlic and herbs, divided
2 – 14.5 ounce cans stewed tomatoes
1/2 teaspoon dried basil
1 clove minced garlic
1 teaspoon dried oregano
1 – 8 ounce package of dried Manicotti shells

Directions:
1. Combine the Ricotta, thawed and squeezed spinach, egg, 1/4 cup of the Parmesan, mozzarella, salt and pepper in a bowl. Set aside
2. In another bowl combine 1 cup of the pasta sauce with one of the cans of stewed tomatoes. Place this combination in the bottom of a nonstick sprayed crock pot
3. Stuff the dry Manicotti shells with the ricotta mixture using your fingers. Be careful not to break the shells. Place a layer of the stuffed Manicotti in the tomato mixture.

4. In the same bowl as before combine the rest of the pasta sauce with the stewed tomatoes. Add the basil, garlic and oregano and mix well. Pour half of it over the stuffed Manicotti and place another layer of stuffed shells on top.
5. Top with the rest of the sauce and top with the other 1/2 cup of Parmesan.
6. Cook covered for 3 to 4 hours and serve immediately.

Crock Pot Macaroni and Cheese
This macaroni and cheese is very creamy and delicious. You don't need to serve anything else with it either because it makes a delicious meal. You can make it into an interesting main course by using it as a macaroni and cheese bar. Fill bowls with cooked bacon, green onions, sliced mushrooms, cooked ham and anything else you want. Guests or family can spoon some macaroni and cheese from the crock pot and top with any of the toppings (or all of them) that they desire.

Ingredients:
4 cups dried elbow macaroni
1 cup sour cream
2 cups milk
4 cups shredded sharp Cheddar cheese
6 tablespoons butter
2 cans Cheddar cheese soup
1/2 teaspoon salt
1/2 teaspoon pepper
3/4 teaspoon dry mustard or 3/4 teaspoon hot sauce

Directions:
1. Boil a large pan of water over high heat and add the macaroni. Boil for about 6 to 8 minutes. The macaroni should still be a bit hard. You wouldn't want to eat it until it is softer, but it will soften up in the Crock pot.
2. Spray a crock pot with nonstick spray. Add the sour cream, milk, 3 cups of the Cheddar cheese, butter that has been cut in several pieces, salt, pepper and mustard or hot sauce. Mix well.
3. Cook covered on low for 20 minutes. Stir to incorporate the butter that has now melted.
4. Cook for about 2 to 3 hours or until there is a light browning of the edges. Add the rest of the Cheddar cheese on top, cover and cook another 15 minutes or until the cheese melts. Serve.

Slow Cooker Cheesy Chicken Pasta
This recipe uses cream cheese and Cheddar to make the chicken cheesy and then it also has dry spaghetti incorporated. It is a deliciously different dish for dinner or for a pot luck where you might want to use a large slow cooker and double the recipe. If your chicken breasts are really thick and large, you might want to cut

them in half lengthwise by placing them on a cutting board, placing a hand on top of the breast and running a sharp knife long ways along the breast. This will ensure that it cooks well.

Ingredients:
1 pound boneless, skinless chicken breasts
2 tablespoons chopped green onion
2 cloves peeled and minced garlic
1/4 teaspoon salt
1/4 teaspoon pepper
3 cups chicken broth
1 – 16 ounce package uncooked spaghetti
1 – 8 ounce package cream cheese
2 cups shredded mild Cheddar cheese

Directions:
1. Spray nonstick spray in a slow cooker and add the chicken breast, green onion, garlic, salt, pepper and the broth.
2. Cover and cook high 4 hours or low 7 to 8 hours
3. Remove the chicken and shred with two forks. Return to the slow cooker.
4. Take the dry spaghetti and break in half. Add to the slow cooker. Cut the cream cheese into small pieces and add to the crock pot along with the shredded cheese. Stir well. If it looks like it could use a little more liquid, add 1/2 cup water.
5. Put the cover back on and cook on high for about 30 more minutes or until the noodles become tender. It make take a little longer.
6. Stir to combine and serve.

Elegant Slow Cooker Risotto
Most people equate risotto with elegant restaurants, but you can have it in your home on your table any time you want, and the best thing about it is you can't ruin it when you cook it in a slow cooker. Risotto is a rice dish that is somewhat difficult to make. Not enough liquid and it is crunchy and too much liquid and it gets squishy. You do need special Arborio rice to make risotto and it is a little expensive, but you don't have to worry about not making it right. Your slow cooker risotto will always be delicious.

Ingredients:
1-1/4 cup uncooked Arborio rice
1/4 cup olive oil
1 teaspoon dried onion flakes
4 cloves of garlic that have been peeled and minced (adjust to your taste)
1/2 teaspoon salt
1/4 teaspoon pepper
1/4 cup dry white wine
3-1/2 cups chicken broth

1 cup grated Parmesan cheese (not out of the shaker box – the real thing)

Directions:
1. Spray the slow cooker with nonstick spray
2. Place the rice and olive oil in the bottom and stir it around making sure to cover the rice with the oil.
3. Add the onion flakes, garlic, salt and pepper and stir
4. Pour in the wine and chicken broth
5. Cover cook on high for 2 hours. The rice should be tender and not crunchy and it might take a little longer than 2 hours.
6. Stir in the grated cheese and turn off the slow cooker. Let it sit 15 minutes uncovered. Stir and serve.

Red Beans and Rice in a Crock Pot

Beans and rice are a staple in Latin cuisine and it has been adopted into many households because it is cheap to make and it is delicious and nutritious. This dish also has sausage in it so it can be made as a main dish. Use smoked sausage of any type including turkey, beef or pork and cut thin slices to put in the dish. The rice is cooked separately and mixed in at the end.

Ingredients:
2 cups dried red kidney beans
1-1/2 cup peeled and chopped yellow or sweet onion
1-1/2 cups seeded and chopped red or green bell pepper
1-1/4 cup chopped celery
4 cloves peeled and minced garlic
1-1/2 teaspoon dried thyme
2 teaspoons paprika
1 teaspoon ground red pepper flakes
1/2 teaspoon black pepper
1/2 teaspoon salt
2 bay leaves
14 ounce package of sausage
3 cups water
3 cups vegetable broth
5 cups cooked long grain rice
3/4 cup chopped green onions

Directions:
1. Spray the slow cooker with nonstick spray and combine the beans, onion, peppers, celery, garlic, thyme, red pepper flakes, black pepper, salt and bay leaves in the bottom.
2. Add the sliced sausage and add the water and broth.
3. Cover and cook on high for 5 hours. Check the tenderness of the beans because it might take a little longer.
4. Remove the bay leaves and serve over the hot cooked rice sprinkled with green onions.

Quinoa in a Crock Pot

Quinoa is a lovely grain that is very nutritious and filling. This dish combines quinoa with a variety of vegetables and other good things like avocado, beans and tomatoes. It will cook up perfectly every time in a crock pot and your family will want it often.

Ingredients:
1 tablespoon olive oil
1 cup peeled and chopped yellow onion
1-1/2 cups seeded and chopped red bell pepper (you can use any color pepper)
3 peeled and minced cloves of garlic
1-1/2 cup dry quinoa
2-1/2 cups vegetable broth
1 – 14.5 ounce can tomatoes with green chilies (do not drain)
1 – 8 ounce can of tomato sauce
1-1/2 teaspoon cumin
1/2 teaspoon salt
1/4 teaspoon pepper
1-1/2 cups frozen corn kernels
1 – 14.5 ounce can black beans that have been drained and rinsed
1 – 14.5 ounce can pinto beans that have been drained and rinsed
1-1/2 cups shredded Monterey Jack or Cheddar cheese
1 avocado diced
3 to 4 Roma tomatoes that have been diced
1/2 cup chopped cilantro
1/2 cup chopped green onion
1 lime cut in wedges

Directions:
1. Heat a large skillet over medium heat. Add olive oil, onions, bell pepper and garlic and sauté for about 3 to 4 minutes. Pour into a nonstick sprayed Crock pot.
2. Stir in the quinoa, broth, canned tomatoes, tomato sauce, chili powder, cumin and salt and pepper.
3. Cover and cook high 3 hours (watch it doesn't start to dry out)
4. Add the frozen corn and beans and stir. Sprinkle the top with cheese. Cover and cook about 15 more minutes
5. Set the avocado, Roma tomatoes, cilantro, green onion and lime wedges in bowls and allow family and guests to add what they wish to their serving.

Crock Pot Couscous with Chicken and Broccoli

Couscous is a fluffy grain that takes on the flavors of the other ingredients in the dish. This dish is filling and delicious and can be used as a side dish or as a main course. It is so easy to make you can't possibly believe it tastes so good, but it is true.

Ingredients:
2 pounds skinless, boneless chicken breasts cut in 2 inch pieces
2 cups chicken broth
1/2 teaspoon salt
1/4 teaspoon pepper
2 cloves peeled and minced garlic
1 cup plain couscous
2 cups frozen broccoli florets

Directions
1. Spray a crock pot with nonstick spray and add the chicken pieces. Pour the broth over top and add the salt, pepper and garlic. Stir to combine.
2. Cover and cook on low for 6 hours or on high for 3 hours
3. Add the broccoli and cook covered for 30 minutes on high.
4. Add the couscous and turn the crock pot off. Stir to combine all ingredients well and put the lid back on for 10 more minutes. Serve once the couscous gets fluffy.

Chapter 7: Top 10 Best Sauce and Condiment Recipes

This chapter is all about sauces and condiments that you can make in your crock pot or slow cooker. It runs the gambit from different pasta sauces, salsa, barbecue sauce, Coney sauce for hot dogs all the way to cranberry sauce and homemade ketchup that is out of this world delicious. You will never buy a bottle of ketchup in the grocery store again. Instead you will tote out the crock pot and make a batch when you need it.

Meaty Spaghetti Sauce
Put the ingredients of this sauce in the crock pot before work and come home to a delicious meal where you only have to cook the noodles and make a salad. The sauce is very chunky with lots of meat and has a very good flavor. I usually get everything cooked up in the skillet and put into the crock pot the night before. When I get out of bed, I run to the kitchen and take it out of the refrigerator so the crock comes more to room temp and before I run out the door 45 minutes to an hour later, I hook it up in the crock pot sleeve and start it up.

Ingredients:
2 tablespoons olive oil
1 large peeled and chopped yellow or sweet onion
1/4 pound Italian sausage (I use mild but you can use hot. Use bulk sausage)
1 pound lean ground beef
1-1/2 teaspoons Italian seasoning
1-1/2 teaspoons dried garlic powder (do not use garlic salt)
1 – 29 ounce can of tomato sauce
1 – 6 ounce can tomato paste
1 – 14.5 ounce can Roma tomatoes that are diced
1 - 14.5 ounce can stewed tomatoes
1/4 teaspoon dried thyme
1/2 teaspoon dried oregano
2 more teaspoons garlic powder
1 tablespoon granulated sugar

Directions:
1. Heat a skillet to medium heat and add the olive oil. Sauté the onions until softened and add the sausage and brown about 10 minutes.
2. Place the onions and sausage in a nonstick sprayed crock pot
3. Brown the ground beef in the same skillet and add the Italian seasoning and garlic powder. Break up and stir for about 10 minutes and place into the crock pot.
4. Pour the tomato sauce, past, diced tomatoes, stewed tomatoes, thyme, basil, oregano and garlic powder in to the crock pot with everything else. Set on low and cook for 8 hours.

5. Just 15 minutes before serving, stir in the sugar and stir well. Serve over spaghetti or another pasta.

Alfredo Sauce in a Slow Cooker

Alfredo sauce is a great change from tomato covered pasta. It is a creamy and buttery cheese sauce that goes well with plain pasta or cheese filled ravioli. This Alfredo sauce is easy to make in a slow cooker. The tendency for it to become grainy when the cheese is added is eliminated because of the slow cooking time. The best thing about Alfredo sauce is that it goes really well with chicken and seafood too. Take the butter out of the refrigerator when you leave in the morning and prepare the crock pot. When you come home the butter is very soft and smooth; the way you want it to be.

Ingredients:
3-1/3 cups chicken broth
2 cups heavy whipping cream
4 peeled and minced cloves of garlic
1/2 cup soft butter
1/2 cup flour
1/4 cup fresh parsley that has been finely chopped
1 cup Parmesan cheese grated from the block

Directions:
1. Spray the inside of the slow cooker.
2. Pour in the broth, cream and add the garlic. Cover and cook low for about 4 to 5 hours.
3. Half hour before serving whisk the butter, flour and parsley in a bowl until it is very smooth. Scrape it into the slow cooker, cover and cook for another 30 minutes. The sauce should thicken.
4. Stir in the grated cheese and let it melt
5. Serve over fettuccine noodles or other pasta

NOTE: If you want to add cooked chicken breast to the sauce, add it during that last 30 minutes after adding the butter mixture. This will heat it through.

Crock Pot Vodka Sauce

Vodka sauce is a pretty light pink creamy tomato sauce with the added punch of vodka. Don't worry about serving it to kids because all the alcohol comes out in the cooking leaving flavor only. Serve over pasta or ravioli for a delightful meal.

Ingredients:
1 small onion that has been peeled and chopped fine
2 cloves peeled and minced garlic
1/2 teaspoon crushed red pepper flakes
1 – 14.5 or 15 ounce can tomato sauce
1 teaspoon olive oil
1 cup beef broth

1 – 14.5 ounce can diced tomatoes (do not drain)
6 basil leaves that have been finely chopped
1 cup vodka
1/2 cup half and half
1/2 teaspoon salt
1/4 teaspoon pepper

Directions:
1. Spray the crock pot with nonstick spray and add all the ingredients except the half and half and salt and pepper.
2. Stir to combine and cover. Cook on low for 6 hours or on high for 4 hours.
3. The last 15 minutes of cooking, whisk the half and half with salt and pepper and add to the crock pot. Whisk all the ingredients, cover and cook on high only for the last 15 minutes
4. Serve over pasta.

Beef and Red Wine Sauce
Have a gourmet meal from your crock pot. Just boil up some egg noodles and serve over top for an elegant meal that is so easy to make, you won't believe it.

Ingredients:
1 tablespoon olive oil
1 medium onion that has been peeled and sliced thin
1 clove peeled and minced garlic
3 pounds boneless beef chuck roast cut into 1 inch pieces
1 pound fresh whole mushrooms that have been cut in half
1 – 1.61 ounce package brown gravy mix
1 – 10.5 ounce can beef broth
1 cup red wine
2 tablespoons tomato paste
1 bay leaf

Directions:
1. Heat a skillet to medium high heat and add the olive oil. Sauté the onion and garlic for about 4 to 5 minutes.
2. Add the beef and brown on all sides
3. Add the mushrooms and sauté another 3 minutes
4. Pour the skillet contents into a crock pot that has been sprayed with nonstick spray
5. Sprinkle over the brown gravy mix and add the beef broth and wine.
6. Add the tomato paste and stir the contents of the crock pot to combine.
7. Add the bay leaf, cover and cook on high for 6 hours
8. Remove the bay leaf and serve the sauce over hot, cooked egg noodles.

Salsa in the Slow Cooker

Salsa is easy to get at the grocery store, but it tastes so much better when you make it yourself and you can do it in a slow cooker. The slow cooking brings out all the flavors to make a dynamite dish. When it cools, put it in a jar and keep in in the refrigerator, if there is any left.

Ingredients:
1 medium peeled and chopped white onion
2 Jalapeño Peppers, seeded and sliced thin
12 Roma tomatoes
4 peeled cloves of garlic
1/4 teaspoon salt
1/4 teaspoon pepper
1 tablespoon fresh lime juice
1/2 cup chopped fresh cilantro

Directions:
1. Place the onions in the bottom of a nonstick sprayed slow cooker.
2. Add the Jalapeño peppers
3. Cut a slit in 4 of the tomatoes and place a clove of garlic in the slit. Add those tomatoes and the rest to the slow cooker
4. Season with salt and pepper and cover. Cook 3 hours on high.
5. Remove the tomatoes from the slow cooker and put in a bowl. Cover with plastic wrap and allow to cool to room temperature. This will loosen the skin. Remove the skin and discard.
6. Put tomatoes and contents of the crock pot in a blender and pulse until you have a chunky consistency. Pour into a bowl and chill for about 2 hours.
7. Add the lime juice and cilantro. Stir and serve

Crock Pot Barbecue Sauce
This sauce is absolutely delicious and made easily in a crock pot. Place some in a mason jar, tie with a ribbon and give to friends as a gift. They won't turn it down and will be asking you for the recipe. Put the ingredients in the crock pot and let it go while you sleep. When you wake up in the morning, turn it off and let it cool down. I use brown mustard in this recipe but you can also use plain mustard. I like the added graininess and flavor it gives to the recipe.

Ingredients:
1 – 28 ounce bottle of ketchup
1 – 12 ounce bottle of beer
1 small onion that has been peeled and chopped fine
1-1/2 cup brown sugar
1/2 cup prepared mustard
2 tablespoons white vinegar
1/2 teaspoon chili powder
1/4 teaspoon cayenne
1/4 teaspoon curry powder

1-1/2 teaspoon garlic powder
1 teaspoon black pepper
1 teaspoon granulated sugar

Directions:
1. Spray a crock pot with nonstick spray
2. Add all the ingredients and stir well
3. Cover and cook on low for 12 hours

NOTE: The sauce will need to be refrigerated after it cools. You can also make big batches and freeze it.

Classic Coney Sauce in A Crock Pot
If you are old enough, you might remember the Coney sauce that was put on hot dogs at stands at fairs or at the beach. Coney sauce has vinegar, ketchup and spices and is also infused with ground beef. It is chunky and delicious. It only takes 2 to 3 hours to cook too, so if you are having a pool party or any other type of party, put it in the crock pot and forget about it for a few hours. Slather it on your hot dogs and enjoy. Keep left overs in the refrigerator or you can freeze this sauce and it comes out good as new when it thaws.

Ingredients:
1 teaspoon olive oil
1 small peeled and chopped onion
1 clove minced garlic
2 pounds ground beef
1-1/2 cups ketchup
1/4 cup granulated sugar
1/4 cup white vinegar
1/4 cup prepared yellow mustard
1/2 teaspoon celery seed
2 drops hot sauce (or to taste if you like it hot)
3/4 teaspoon Worcestershire sauce
1/4 teaspoon salt
1/4 teaspoon pepper

Directions:
1. Place the olive oil in a heated skillet over medium heat. Add the onion and garlic and sauté until tender, about 4 minutes. Add the ground beef and cook until it is completely browned. Drain any grease off.
2. Place the beef mixture in a crock pot sprayed with nonstick spray and add the rest of the ingredients.
3. Cover and cook on low for about 3 hours.

Homemade Crock Pot Ketchup
Did you know you can make your own ketchup and you can make it in a crock pot. Use this ketchup in the other recipes in this chapter or just have it on hand

to serve with meatloaf, fries or other things you flavor with ketchup It is so easy to make, you may never buy another bottle of commercial ketchup again. This does need to be refrigerated, but it lasts quite a long time if there is any left to save. It is best to used peeled tomatoes, but if you can't find those, use regular ones. The blender should chop up the skins pretty well and you do strain it. It is just easier to use the peeled brand.

Ingredients:
2 – 28 ounce cans peeled tomatoes (sometimes stewed tomatoes are peeled)
1/2 cup water
2/3 cup granulated sugar
3/4 cup white vinegar
1 teaspoon onion powder
1/2 teaspoon garlic powder
1/2 teaspoon salt
1/8 teaspoon celery salt
1/8 teaspoon mustard powder
1/4 teaspoon ground pepper
1/4 teaspoon cayenne pepper
1 whole clove

Directions:
1. Spray a crock pot with nonstick spray
2. Pour in the tomatoes. Divide the water between the 2 tomato cans and swirl to get all the tomatoes out of the can. Pour into the crock pot. Use a whisk to combine all together.
3. Add the rest of the ingredients, cover and cook on high for 6 hours, stirring once every hour. Remove the lid and cook 6 more hours, stirring every hour. The mixture should get very thick.
4. Remove the clove.
5. Use an immersion blender to blend everything smooth or put the mixture in a regular blender and blend until smooth.
6. Ladle the mixture into a fine strainer to strain out any peels or seeds that might be left in. Use the back of the ladle to force it through the strainer into a container. Cool completely and put in bottles or jars and refrigerate.

Slow Cooker Apple Butter
I love homemade bread slathered with apple butter for breakfast. Old fashion apple butter takes a long time and trouble to make, but this slow cooker version is pretty easy and tastes remarkably like the type stirred over a fire in a cast iron pot. It does take all day to make, but it is really worth it. You can give this apple butter as gifts to friends and family, but it does need to be refrigerated. Depending on how sweet the apples are that are used, the sugar can be adjusted to more or less once you get the hang of making it.

Ingredients:
5-1/2 pounds apples (I use Macintosh apples)

4 cups granulated sugar
2-1/2 teaspoon cinnamon
1/2 teaspoon ground cloves
1/4 teaspoon salt

Directions:
1. Peel, core and slice the apples placing them in a slow cooker that has been sprayed with nonstick spray
2. Mix the sugar, cinnamon, cloves and salt in a small bowl and pour over the apples. Toss well to coat all the apple slices.
3. Cover and cook on high for 1 hour
4. Reduce heat to low and cook for another 10 hours, stirring every hour or so it doesn't stick. The mixture should thicken.
5. Take the cover off and cook another hour. This should thicken up the apple butter significantly.
6. Once cooled, spoon into jars or freezer containers. Keep it refrigerated or freeze.

Slow Cooker Cranberry Sauce

If you put this on Thanksgiving morning, you whole house will smell delicious once guests start to arrive for dinner. This cranberry sauce is chunky and delicious One thing I did learn is to stir it every so often to make sure it doesn't burn on the edges, but it takes less time than cooking the turkey to make it. I like to call it my 1/2 cup cranberry sauce. The recipe is easy to remember because everything is in 1/2 cup increments except the cinnamon and orange peel, which are 1/2 teaspoonful, and the package of cranberries.

Ingredients:
1/2 cup water
1/2 cup orange juice
1/2 cup granulated sugar
1/2 cup packed brown sugar
1/2 teaspoon ground cinnamon
1/2 teaspoon grated orange peel
1 – 12 ounce package fresh cranberries

Directions:
1. Spray the slow cooker with nonstick spray.
2. Measure the water and orange juice into the slow cooker.
3. Add both sugars and whisk with a wire whisk
4. Add the cinnamon and orange peel and whisk again
5. Add the cranberries, cover and cook on high for 3 hours, stirring at least every hour.
6. Remove the lid and continue to cook on high until all the cranberries pop and the sauce thickens. This could take anywhere from 30 to 60 minutes.
7. Cool before serving. Keep leftovers refrigerated.

Chapter 8: Top 10 Best Breakfast and Lunch Recipes

The following recipes are suitable for either breakfast or lunch and all are made in a crock pot. They are also interchangeable, in fact, you can really use them for a light dinner too. They are perfect for brunch because most of them only take a few hours to cook. This is enough to feed a large family.

Sausage and Eggs in a Crock Pot

This recipe only takes about 3 hours on high. Use bulk sausage instead of links or patties and you can use either hot or sweet sausage. You can have this ready and on the table in 3 hours at low or 5 at high. I do not suggest putting it in overnight as it will get overdone.

Ingredients:
1 – 20 ounce bag of frozen hash browns that are thawed and drained
1 pound bulk sausage
12 eggs
3/4 cup half and half
1/2 teaspoon red pepper flakes that have been crushed
1/2 teaspoon salt
1/4 teaspoon pepper
1/2 cup chopped green onion
1/2 cup seeded and chopped red pepper
2 cups shredded Cheddar (you can use Monterey Jack or Swiss to switch it up)

Directions:
1. Thaw the frozen hash browns and drain. You might want to squeeze between paper towels to get out as much moisture as possible. Set aside.
2. Brown the sausage well and drain. Set aside.
3. Whisk the eggs in a bowl and add the red pepper flakes, salt and pepper. Whisk again.
4. Chop your onion and red pepper and place in a bowl. Reserve 2 tablespoons of the chopped onions in another small bowl. Set both bowls aside.
5. Place half of the hash browns in the bottom of a nonstick sprayed crock pot. Layer with half the sausage and half the pepper and green onion combination. Sprinkle half of the cheese on top.
6. Do another layer of hash browns, sausage, pepper and green onions. Layer on half of the cheese you have left and reserve the rest.
7. Carefully pour the egg mixture over top everything and cover and cook 4 to 5 hours on low or 2-1/2 to 3 hours on high. It is done when you put a meat thermometer in and it registers at 160 degrees F.
8. Sprinkle the rest of the cheese and green onions over top before serving.

Egg, Spinach and Ham Crock Pot Dish

If you have extra ham left over from a meal, this makes a great breakfast dish the next day. It only takes a little over 2 hours to make and is filled with goodness.

Ingredients:
6 eggs
1/2 teaspoon salt
1/4 teaspoon pepper
1/2 cup Greek yogurt
1/4 cup milk
1/2 teaspoon thyme
1 clove minced garlic
1/2 medium onion that has been peeled and chopped
1/3 cup cleaned and diced mushrooms
1 cup baby spinach packed
1 cup shredded pepper jack cheese
1 cup cooked, diced ham

Directions:
1. Whisk the eggs in a very large bowl. Everything is going to go in the bowl before it goes into the crock pot.
2. Add the salt, pepper, yogurt, milk and thyme and mix well.
3. Add the garlic, onion, mushrooms, spinach, cheese and ham and mix well.
4. Pour into a nonstick sprayed crock pot and cook on high for 90 minutes to 2 hours or until the mixture becomes set. Slice and serve.

Slow Cooker Huevos Rancheros
This Mexican inspired egg dish can be served just as it is or get 8 corn tortillas and serve on them with avocado, green onion, cilantro and a little lime juice. Just roll it up and enjoy or slice in wedges and eat with a fork, garnishing with a little chopped green onion.

Ingredients:
10 eggs
1 cup half and half
12 ounces shredded Monterey Jack cheese
1/2 teaspoon pepper
1/2 teaspoon chili powder
1 clove minced garlic
1 – 4 ounce can of chopped green chili
1 – 10 ounce bottle salsa or homemade salsa

Directions:
1. Whisk the eggs in a large bowl and add in the half and half and half of the cheese. Whisk well.
2. Add the pepper, chili powder, garlic and green chilies.
3. Pour into a nonstick sprayed slow cooker, cover and cook on low for 2 hours.

4. Serve in wedges on a plate or on top of a corn tortilla. Top with salsa and sprinkle cheese over.

Chocolate Chip French Toast

This is a perfect brunch dish. It takes about 4 hours to cook on low and I've tried on high, but it always seems to get too toasty that way, even at half the time. You need to refrigerate the mixture over night and put it in the crock pot cold. We serve this on Christmas morning. I make it the night before and put the whole crock pot in the refrigerator. I get up at about 5 and put it on and we are ready to chow down at 9 after the presents have been opened.

Ingredients:
1 pound French bread that has been cut in 1 inch cubes
3 eggs
1-1/2 cup milk
3/4 cup packed brown sugar
1 teaspoon cinnamon
1 teaspoon vanilla
1 cup semisweet chocolate chips

Directions:
1. Spray a crock pot with nonstick spray and place the French bread cubes in the bottom.
2. Whisk the eggs and milk in a large bowl. Add the sugar, cinnamon and vanilla and mix well.
3. Pour the egg mixture over the bread, cover and put in refrigerator overnight.
4. Sprinkle with chocolate chips, cover and cook on low for 4 hours.

Cinnamon Apple Oatmeal

You can make this the night before providing you do not leave it going more than 7 hours. On high it takes about 3 hours to cook and it is the best oatmeal you ever tasted.

Ingredients:
1-1/2 cups coconut milk
1-1/2 cups water
2 peeled, cored and diced apples
2 tablespoons brown sugar
1 tablespoon coconut oil
1 teaspoon cinnamon
1/4 teaspoon salt
1 cup Steel Cut oats
chopped nuts as garnish

Directions:

1. Spray a crock pot with nonstick spray.
2. Add all ingredients and stir.
3. Cook covered on low for 5 to 7 hours and high 3 hours.
4. Top with nuts before serving.

Rump Roast Beef Sandwich
You make the filling in the crock pot for about 8 hours and shred the meat. Serve over Kaiser rolls and add a little provolone cheese if desired.

Ingredients:
1 – 3 to 4 pound beef rump roast
1 – can cream of mushroom soup
1 envelope onion soup mix
2 ribs celery that have been chopped fine
1 – 6 ounce jar of sliced mushrooms that have been drained well

Directions:
1. Spray the inside of a crock pot. Cut the roast to fit inside if necessary.
2. Mix in a bow the soup, soup mix, celery and pour over the roast.
3. Cover and cook for 8 to 10 hours on low.
4. One hour before serving, remove the meat from the crock pot and let it cool about 10 minutes. Take two forks and shred the meat. Return it to the crock pot along with the drained mushrooms.
5. Cook until everything is heated through and put 1/2 cup on each roll.

Hot and Delicious Ham Sandwiches
Put the filling for this sandwich on in the morning and it will be ready for lunch. This is more than a ham sandwich because it has pickles, apple juice and the smoky flavor of paprika included. It is great for parties or for the family.

Ingredients:
3 pounds of thin sliced deli ham
2/3 cup packed brown sugar
1/2 cup sweet pickle relish
1 teaspoon paprika
2 teaspoons prepared brown or yellow mustard
2 cups apple juice

Directions:
1. Spray the inside of a crock pot with nonstick spray
2. Separate the ham slices and place them in the crock pot one by one
3. Mix in a bowl the brown sugar, pickle relish, paprika and mustard. Add the apple juice and mix thoroughly.
4. Pour the mixture in the bowl over top of the ham in the crock pot.
5. Cover and cook low for 4 to 5 hours
6. Place 3 to 4 slices of the ham on a Kaiser roll and top with more pickle relish if desired.

Rustic Chicken Sandwich in a Slow Cooker

You cook the chicken in the crock pot, take it out and shred it and return it to the crock pot. This makes a tasty sandwich for lunch or dinner that has the flavor of pesto. Serve it on Kaiser rolls or on some focaccia.

Ingredients:
1-1/4 pound boneless chicken thighs
1/2 cup roasted red bell pepper (from a jar or roast yourself and chop)
2 cloves minced garlic
1/2 teaspoon salt
1/4 cup mayonnaise
3 tablespoons pesto
Sliced tomatoes

Directions:
1. Place the whole thighs in a nonstick sprayed crock pot and sprinkle over the garlic and chopped peppers.
2. Cover and cook on low for 6 to 7 hours or on high for 4 hours
3. Remove the chicken and shred with two forks. Return the chicken to the crock pot and heat through
4. Mix the mayonnaise and pesto in a bowl.
5. Cut focaccia in wedges and split them in half or use Kaiser rolls
6. Spread with the mayonnaise mixture and with a slotted spoon, place about 1/3 cup of the chicken filling on top. Top with a slice of tomato and serve.

Philly Inspired Cheese Sandwich in a Slow Cooker

Use a pot roast to make this delicious sandwich that tastes much like the ones you get in Philadelphia. They have the meat, cheese, onions and peppers and taste delicious on a hoagie bun

Ingredients:
2-1/2 pound boneless beef chuck pot roast
1 cup peeled and chopped onion
1/4 cup Worcestershire sauce
1/2 cup beef broth
2 peeled and minced cloves of garlic
1 teaspoon dried oregano
1/2 teaspoon dried basil
1/2 teaspoon dried thyme
1 cup pickled peppers, or sautéed red or green bell peppers
Slices of Provolone cheese

Directions:
1. Trim the fat from the pot roast and slice the roast in thin strips. Place the strips in a slow cooker that has been sprayed with nonstick spray.

2. Add the onion, Worcestershire sauce, beef broth, garlic and all the herbs to the crock pot. If you are using bell peppers, put them in now too. If you are using pickled peppers, wait to add those later.
3. Cover and cook on low 10 to 12 hours or on high 5 to 6 hours. Stir occasionally to keep the meat from clumping together.
4. During the last 30 minutes, add the pickled peppers if you are using them.
5. Toast the hoagie buns under the broiler until brown. Remove and top with the meat mixture and a couple slices of Provolone Put back under the broiler until the cheese melts and serve.

Italian Sausage and Pepper Sandwiches

Why wait for the county fair to come to have these delicious sandwiches. Use bulk sweet, hot or mild Italian sausage for best results. This filling smells so good, you might have the whole neighborhood at your door throughout the cooking process.

Ingredients:
1 teaspoon olive oil
1 large peeled and thin sliced onion
20 ounces of Italian sausage
2 large red bell peppers that have been seeded and sliced in strips
1 large green bell pepper that has been seeded and sliced in strips
1 large yellow bell pepper that has been seeded and sliced in strips
1/4 cup red wine vinegar
1/2 teaspoon pepper
1/2 teaspoon thyme
1-1/2 tablespoon cornstarch
2 tablespoons water
1 teaspoon prepared brown mustard
hoagie rolls
slices of Provolone cheese

Directions:
1. Heat a skillet to medium high heat and pour in the olive oil. Sauté the onion for 3 minutes and add the sausage and just brown it. Remove with a slotted spoon and drain on paper towels.
2. Spray a crock pot with nonstick spray
3. Place the onion and meat mixture in the crock pot. Add the vinegar, pepper, thyme and cook covered on high 3 hours or on low 6 hours
4. Remove the solids from the crock pot and put in a bowl. Pour out the liquid into a saucepan.
5. Combine the cornstarch with the water and add to the liquids. Whisk in the mustard and boil about 1 minute, stirring constantly or until thickened.
6. Place the bottoms and top of the hoagie buns on a broiler pan and toast for about 1 or 2 minutes. Remove the tops.

7. Divide the filling in the bowl between all the hoagie buns. Drizzle with the juice in the sauce pan and apply Provolone cheese. Place under the broiler until the cheese melts. Top and serve.

Chapter 9: Top 10 Best Appetizer Recipes

Appetizers are a good way to get the appetite going and those digestive juices flowing. Just a little something before a meal holds you over until it is served. I like to serve appetizers during holidays when you may skip the noon lunch and go for a 2 o'clock serving of dinner. They keep the body and soul on speaking terms until dinner is served without stuffing the stomach. Think about having only appetizers at your next party or you can opt for appetizers and sandwiches. The following appetizers include dips. Some of the dips are hot dips that you serve right out of the crock pot. Use crackers, small rye rounds, pita chips, potato chips and pretzels to accompany the dips. The rest of the recipes are other types of appetizers like wings or meatballs that are perfect for that "little" something.

Crock Pot Hot Crab Dip
This recipe uses canned flaked crab so all you have to do is pour everything into the crock pot and let it go. It is delicious served with crackers or pita chips.

Ingredients:
2 – 8 ounce packages of cream cheese that is softened
3/4 cup mayonnaise
3/4 cup Parmesan Cheese shredded from a block
1-1/2 tablespoons Worcestershire Sauce
1/4 cup green onions that have been sliced very thin
2 – 6 ounce cans of crab flaked crab meat with cartilage removed, drained well
Fresh chives

Directions:
1. Spray the inside of the crock pot with nonstick spray.
2. Mix the softened cream cheese, mayonnaise, Parmesan, Worcestershire sauce and green onions in a bowl. Use a fork to work the mixture together very well.
3. Pour the mixture into the crock pot, cover and cook on low 2 hours. Put it on the warm setting and serve from the crock pot with chives sprinkled on top.

Crock Pot Pale Ale Garden Dip
Those that like the flavor of pale ale will love this recipe. There are all kinds of good things from vegetables, to herbs and spices, to cheese and bacon – not to mention the pale ale. This goes well with tortilla chips.

Ingredients:
1/2 teaspoon ground cumin
1/2 teaspoon chili powder
1/2 teaspoon onion powder
1/4 teaspoon salt
1/4 teaspoon pepper
3/4 cup sour cream

12 ounces softened cream cheese
3-1/2 cups frozen corn kernels
1 minced jalapeño pepper with seeds and stem removed
1 diced red bell pepper with seed and stem removed
2 cloves peeled and minced garlic
1-1/2 cup shredded Monterey Jack cheese
1/2 cup pale ale beer
5 strips bacon
green onions

Directions:
1. Combine the cumin, chili powder, onion powder, salt and pepper in a small bowl. Set aside.
2. In another bowl combine the sour cream and cream cheese and add the herbs and spices. Mix in with a fork to get it well combined.
3. Spray the inside of the crock pot with nonstick spray and place the corn, both peppers and Monterey Jack cheese inside.
4. Add the herb and cream cheese mixture to the crock pot and pour the ale over top.
5. Cook covered for 6 to 8 hours on low or 4 to 5 hours on high.
6. In the meantime, cook bacon, drain on paper towels and let it cool. Break it into small pieces.
7. Chop the chives for garnish.
8. Stir everything together before serving and sprinkle on the bacon and chives.

Slow Cooker Buffalo Chicken Dip
This dip is a favorite in our family. We like cold or hot and it goes well with tortilla chips, crackers, pita chips or bagel chips. We actually use it as a filling for a sandwich between rye bread.

Ingredients:
16 ounces cream cheese that has been cut into cubes and softened
1/4 cup hot sauce (you can add more or less depending on taste)
1 cup prepared ranch dressing
2 cups chicken that has been cooked and shredded (I use breasts)
2 cups shredded sharp Cheddar cheese

Directions:
1. Spray the slow cooker with nonstick spray
2. Mix the cream cheese, hot sauce and ranch dressing in a bowl until well combined. Pour into the crock pot
3. Cook on low for 2 hours stirring every 1/2 hour or so
4. Add the chicken and cheddar and cook 1 more hour stirring at least twice so the cheese does not burn.
5. Put on warm and serve from the slow cooker.

Slow Cooker Pepperoni Dip

This is a simple, yet delicious dip that is very spicy and flavorful. It doesn't really look like the ingredients go together, but once you taste it, you will change your mind. This is good on whole wheat crackers or on bread.

Ingredients:
7 ounces of sliced pepperoni
8 ounces softened cream cheese
1 – 10.5 ounce cream of celery soup

Directions:
1. Spray nonstick spray in the crock pot
2. Cut pepperoni slices in half and put into the crock pot
3. Cut the cream cheese into chunks and put on top of the pepperoni
4. Scrape the soup out of the can and spread on top.
5. Cover and cook on low about 1 hour, stirring every once in a while. Keep on warm to serve.

Slow Cooker Hot Onion Dip

Use wavy chips with this dip because you will want to pile it on it is so good. It also goes well with little bread rounds, pita or bagel chips and pretzels. I'm salivating and need to go make some now.

Ingredients:
1 teaspoon olive oil
1 medium onion that has been peeled and chopped fine
16 ounces cubed and softened cream cheese
1-1/2 cups shredded or grated Parmesan Cheese (only use fresh cheese, not the stuff in the can)

Directions:
1. Heat a skillet to medium high heat and add the olive oil. Add the onion and sauté for about 3 to 4 minutes.
2. Spray the slow cooker with nonstick spray and add the onion
3. Add the cream cheese and Parmesan
4. Cook covered for about 2 hours stirring every half hour and serve keeping the dip warm.

NOTE: This is a versatile dip. You can add some cooked bacon, chives, garlic and anything else you think might taste good. Do that at the end when there is only about 15 more minutes for it to cook.

Slow Cooked Wings

This recipe makes the best sweet and spicy chicken wings ever. It has lemon juice, chili sauce, molasses and salsa to name a few things and it will soon become a favorite at football gathers and other parties.

Ingredients:
5 to 6 pounds chicken wings that have been split and tips removed
1 – 12 ounce bottle chili sauce
1 tablespoon commercial salsa
1/4 cup molasses
1-1/2 tablespoon Worcestershire sauce
1/4 cup fresh squeezed lemon juice
3 drops hot sauce (more or less as desired)
1 teaspoon garlic powder
1/4 teaspoon salt
2 teaspoons chili powder

Directions:
1. Place the wings in a nonstick sprayed slow cooker
2. In a bowl, combine the chili sauce, salsa, molasses, Worcestershire sauce, lemon juice, hot sauce, garlic powder, salt and chili powder and mix well.
3. Pour over the wings and cook on low for 5 hours and serve.

Crock Pot Sweet and Spicy Kielbasa
Kielbasa is also called Polish Sausage and is a pork product (although you can find beef varieties) that are in a large link and it is very fragrant and spicy. It needs to be sliced in thin coins for this recipe and then goes in with brown sugar and a few other ingredients and almost gets a candy coating. It is really good!

Ingredients:
1/2 cup ketchup
1/4 cup horseradish
1 cup packed brown sugar
2 pounds kielbasa, sliced in thin coins

Directions:
1. Spray a crock pot with nonstick spray. Do not skip this because the ingredients will set up and be very hard to get off once it cools.
2. Whisk together the ketchup and horseradish in a bowl. Add the brown sugar and mix well.
3. Place the sliced kielbasa in the crock pot and pour the sauce over top. Stir lightly.
4. Put the lid on and cook on high until the mixture starts to boil on the sides. Reduce to low and cook about 1 hour or until the sauce thickens.

Slow Cooker Marinated Mushrooms
These mushrooms are tender and delicious and you just put them in the crock pot and cook for about 8 hours; in time for an evening party.

Ingredients:

1 cup chicken broth
1 cup beef broth
1 cup dry red wine
1 teaspoon Worcestershire sauce
1 teaspoon dill
1 teaspoon garlic powder
4 pounds fresh mushrooms
1/2 cup butter

Directions:
1. Place the broths and red wine in a sauce pan and bring to a boil
2. Add the Worcestershire sauce, dill and garlic powder and stir to combine.
3. Remove the stems from the mushrooms and chop
4. Place the mushrooms on the bottom of a nonstick sprayed crock pot and sprinkle the chopped stems over top
5. Pour the broth mixture over top and top with the butter.
6. Cook on low for about 8 hours and serve.

Crock Pot Ham Meatballs
Want something a little different than beef meatballs? Try some ham balls with cranberry. These meatballs are crimson in color and deliciously different.

Ingredients:
1 beaten egg
1/4 cup peeled and finely chopped onion
2 tablespoons dried cranberries cut into small pieces with scissors
1/2 cup pulverized graham crackers
2 tablespoons milk
1/4 teaspoon ground cloves
12 ounces ground pork
12 ounces ground fully cooked ham
1 teaspoon olive oil
1 -16 ounce can jellied cranberry sauce
1 tablespoon vinegar
1 – 12 ounce bottle chili sauce
1/2 teaspoon dry mustard

Directions:
1. In a bowl, beat the egg. Add the onion, cranberries, graham cracker crumbs, milk, cloves, pork and ham. Mix well with the hands and form into small meatballs. It will make about 75.
2. Brown the meatballs in olive oil in a skillet over medium heat. Cook them almost all the way through. Remove and drain on paper towels
3. Combine the cranberry sauce, vinegar, chili sauce and mustard in a sauce pan and heat over medium heat. Keep cooking until cranberry sauce melts and the mixture becomes smooth

4. Spray a crock pot with nonstick spray and place the drained meatballs in the bottom. Pour the sauce over top.
5. Cover and cook on high for 3 hours. Reduce to warm and serve.

Crock Pot Nachos
Nachos are a favorite snack so put this on when you know the family is going to have a movie night or serve at your next gathering.

Ingredients:
1 teaspoon salt
1 tablespoon garlic powder
1 tablespoon cumin
1 tablespoon chili powder
1 teaspoon pepper
1 small peeled and chopped onion
1 – 4 ounce can green chilies drained and diced
1 – canned Chipotle pepper that has been chopped
5 cups chicken broth
4 pounds boneless and skinless chicken thighs
1 tablespoon granulated sugar
1 tablespoon water
Tortilla chips
Shredded cheddar cheese
Lettuce
Olives
Diced tomatoes
Sour cream

Directions:
1. In a small bowl combine the salt, garlic powder, cumin, chili powder and pepper. Set aside
2. Spray a crock pot with nonstick spray and place the onion, green chilies and Chipotle pepper in the bottom.
3. Pour over the chicken broth.
4. Rub the chicken with some of the salt mixture reserving about 1 tablespoon. Place the chicken in the crock pot.
5. Cook covered on high for 6 hours and low for 8 hours
6. Remove the chicken and shred with two forks
7. Place tortilla chips on a large platter
8. Layer on 2 cups of the shredded chicken, shredded Cheddar and any of the other toppings or ones you come up with on top
9. In a small bowl combine the rest of the seasoning mix with the sugar and water. Mix well and drizzle over the Nachos
10. Serve with sour cream.

Chapter 10: Top 10 Best Deserts and Treats

I had a friend that made the most wonderful deserts right in her dorm room using a crock pot. You too can make some delicious creations for deserts and snacks right in your crock pot. When my oven went on the fritz, I had planned on having friends over for snacks and desert. Most people would have gone into a fit about that, but I had my trusty crock pot dessert and sweet treat recipes to fall back on. Now they are part of the family's life and we make them frequently.

Chocolate Mocha Cake in a Crock Pot
If you make this right, the middle stays a little loose. It is supposed to be served warm so that does happen. It is really chocolaty with that mocha flavor and is great served with ice cream, or with whipped cream and sliced raspberries on top. There is no frosting, but it is sweet enough to be delicious without it.

Ingredients:
4 large eggs
1/2 cup melted butter
1-1/2 cup granulated sugar
3 teaspoons vanilla
1 cup flour
1/2 cup powdered cocoa
1/4 teaspoon salt
1 tablespoon instant coffee

Directions:
1. Beat the eggs in a large bowl with a hand mixer and add butter, sugar and vanilla. Beat well.
2. Measure out the flour, cocoa salt and coffee into another bowl and whisk it all together until it is well combined
3. Gradually add the flour mixture to the egg mixture, beating well after each addition.
4. Scrape the batter into a crock pot that has been sprayed well with nonstick baking spray. Use one of the 1-1/2 quart crock pots for this because it spreads out too thin in a large crock pot and will burn.
5. Cover and cook on low for 3 hours. Check the cake with a toothpick or sharp knife in the middle. If it comes out with moist crumbs and no liquid, it is done. Serve by scooping out portions while the cake is still warm.

Slow Cooker Chocolate Extreme Cake
If you love chocolate, you will love this cake. There is chocolate cake mix, chocolate pudding and chocolate chips in it making it very chocolaty and delicious. Serve it with whipped cream or ice cream. This cake is also without any frosting, but that might be a little too much sweetness for one recipe anyway.

Ingredients
1 regular sized chocolate cake mix

1 – 3.9 ounce package of instant chocolate pudding mix
3/4 cup vegetable oil
1 cup water
4 large eggs, slightly beaten
1 – 16 ounce container of sour cream
1 – 6 ounce package of semisweet chocolate chips

Directions:
1. Place the cake mix and pudding mix in a bowl and whisk well together.
2. In a mixer bowl combine the oil, water and eggs, beating until frothy. Beat in the sour cream and gradually add the cake mix mixture beating in well.
3. Hand stir in the chocolate chips.
4. Pour into a 5 quart slow cooker. This is too much for a small slow cooker; it will never finish cooking, so use a large one.
5. Cover and cook on low for 6 to 8 hours. Check by inserting a toothpick or sharp knife in the center. If it comes out with moist crumbs and isn't gooey, the cake is done.
6. Serve warm in bowls with whipped cream over top.

Slow Cooker Pineapple Upside Down Cake
This recipe is easy to make, just be sure you have the muscles to invert the crock pot over a plate to make the cake come out the way it should. It is made in a 5 - 1/2 or 6 quart slow cooker and you actually remove the ceramic bowl from the base and turn it upside down to release the cake. It is certainly worth all the trouble as this cake is moist and delicious.

Ingredients:
1 cup packed brown sugar
1/4 cup melted butter
1 – 20 ounce can pineapple slices in juice
10 – maraschino cherries drained with stems removed
1 cup combination of juice from the pineapple and water
1 regular box yellow super moist cake mix
Vegetable oil as called for with the cake mix
Eggs as called for with the cake mix

Directions:
1. Combine the brown sugar and melted butter in a bowl.
2. Spray a slow cooker with nonstick baking spray well on the bottom and up the sides.
3. Spread the sugar and butter mixture evenly across the bottom of the slow cooker.
4. Pour the pineapple juice from the can of slices into a 1 cup measuring cup and reserve.
5. Place the pineapple slices over the sugar and butter mixture. You may have to cut some of the pineapple slices to fit in the oval, but you should cover the entire bottom.

6. Place the cherries in the holes where the core was in the pineapple slices.
7. Add enough water to the pineapple juice to make one cup and set aside.
8. Mix up the cake mix as per the directions on the package using vegetable oil and eggs. Instead of adding the water listed on the package directions, use the 1 cup juice and water combination. Beat well.
9. Spread the cake batter over top the pineapple slices and cherries evenly.
10. Cook on high for 2-1/2 to 3 hours or until a sharp knife or toothpick inserted in the center comes on clean. Turn the slow cooker off and take the ceramic bowl from the base and place it on a cooling rack for 15 minutes
11. Place a heatproof platter upside down over the opening of the ceramic bowl of the slow cooker and carefully turn it upside down. The cake should fall out onto the platter. Remove the ceramic base and serve warm.

Slow Cooker Sour Cream Cheese Cake
Yes, you can make cheesecake in a slow cooker and it comes out creamy and luscious. You will need a metal 6 inch spring form pan that is 3 inches deep to make this recipe and a large oval slow cooker. You will also have to have a rack that fits into the bottom of the slow cooker.

Ingredients:
3/4 cup fine graham cracker crumbs
1 tablespoon granulated sugar
1/4 teaspoon cinnamon
1 pinch salt
2-1/2 tablespoons melted unsalted butter
2/3 cup more granulated sugar
1/4 teaspoon salt
2 large eggs
1 teaspoon almond extract
1 cup sour cream

Directions:
1. Mix the graham cracker crumbs, 1 tablespoon granulated sugar, cinnamon and salt in a medium bowl. Add the melted butter and mix with a fork.
2. Pres the mixture into the bottom and 1 inch up the sides of a spring form pan that has been sprayed with nonstick spray.
3. Use your mixer with a paddle and combine the cream cheese with flour, 2/3 cup sugar and 1/4 teaspoon salt. Beat until smooth.
4. Scrape down the sides of the bowl and add the eggs and almond extract, beating until smooth
5. Add the sour cream and beat until well incorporated.
6. Pour the batter into the spring form pan
7. Fill the slow cooker with 1/2 inch water on the bottom and place a rack in the bottom.

8. Cover the opening of the slow cooker with a triple layer of paper towels and fit the cover over top holding them up so they don't fall into the cheesecake. Cook on high for 2 hours
9. Do not lift the lid or paper towels. Turn off the slow cooker and let stand for about 1 hour.
10. Remove the lid and towels and pull out the spring form pan. Place it on a cooling rack for 1 hour. Cover with plastic wrap and put it in the refrigerator at least 4 hours.
11. Heat a sharp knife with hot water and dry it off. Run it around the edge of the spring form pan. Release the spring and life the sides off. Cut wedges to serve.

Crock Pot Rice Pudding

Rice pudding is a comfort food in my house. It is creamy, sweet and delicious. It is particularly good for anyone that is recovering from a virus once they can actually eat food again, but we like to serve any time of the year.

Ingredients:
1/2 cup sugar
1/2 cup uncooked rice (Use converted rice)
1/2 cup raisins
1-1/4 cups milk (2% is fine to use)
2 lightly beaten eggs
1 teaspoon melted butter
1 teaspoon cinnamon
1-1/2 teaspoon vanilla
1/2 teaspoon lemon extract (optional – it gives some brightness to the dish)
1 cup heavy whipping cream that has been whipped up (make a little more for garnish)

Directions:
1. Spray a 1-1/2 quart crock pot with nonstick spray
2. Combine together in a bowl the sugar, rice, raisins, milk, beaten eggs, cinnamon, vanilla and lemon extract and lightly mix together. Pour into the crock pot.
3. Cover and cook on low for about 2 hours. Stir and place the lid back on and cook another hour or until the rice is soft and tender.
4. Transfer the pudding to a bowl and let it cool for about 1 hour. Place it covered in the refrigerator until chilled.
5. Whip the heavy cream right before serving and fold it in to the cold pudding. You can garnish with more whipped cream and a shake of cinnamon.

Bread Pudding a la Slow Cooker

Use up your stale white bread or opt for getting French Bread and letting it sit out overnight so it gets hard. This bread pudding is cinnamon flavored and delicious and is a really good way to use up bread that would not normally be used. Use a large, oval 5 quarter slow cooker for this recipe as it makes more than a small one can handle.

Ingredients:
8 cups stale white bread or day old French bread cut in 1 inch cubes
1/2 cup golden raisins
4 eggs
2 cups milk
1/4 cup melted butter
1 cup granulated sugar
1 teaspoon cinnamon
1/4 teaspoon nutmeg
1/8 teaspoon salt
1/2 teaspoon vanilla extract

Directions:
1. Spray the inside of the crock pot with nonstick baking spray.
2. Place the bread cubes and raisins in the bottom
3. Lightly beat the eggs in a large bowl and add the milk and melted butter and whisk together well.
4. In another bowl combine the sugar, cinnamon, nutmeg and salt. Whisk to combine well.
5. Add the sugar mixture to the egg mixture beating well. Add the vanilla and beat to combine all together.
6. Pour over the bread and raisins and toss well to combine and distribute evenly over the slow cooker.
7. Cover and cook on low for about 3 hours or until a toothpick or sharp knife inserted into the center comes out clean.
8. Serve this dessert warm with some whipped cream over top.

Crock Pot Apple Crisp
This recipe tastes spicy just like grandma's recipe that was baked in the oven. You do not have to even peel the apples for this dish. If you don't like the peels, feel free to get rid of them because it is good either way.

Ingredients:
1/2 cup granulated sugar
1/2 teaspoon ground cinnamon
6 cups cored and sliced apples
1 cup Bisquick mix
1/2 cup quick cooking oatmeal
1/4 cup granulated sugar
1/3 cup packed brown sugar
1/4 teaspoon salt
1/4 teaspoon nutmeg
1/4 teaspoon cinnamon

1/2 cup cold butter that has been cut into small pieces

Directions:
1. Combine the sugar and cinnamon in a medium bowl
2. Add the apples and toss to coat all the apples with the sugar and cinnamon mixture.
3. Spray a 5 quart crock pot with nonstick baking spray. Pour the apple mixture in the bottom.
4. In another bowl combine the Bisquick, oatmeal, 1/4 cup sugar, brown sugar, salt, nutmeg and cinnamon. Whisk to combine well and place the butter on top. Use a pastry blender or fork to cut the butter in and make the mixture crumbly.
5. Sprinkle over the apples, cover and cook on high for 3 hours. Watch that the crisp doesn't get too brown around the edges.
6. Serve warm in bowls topped by whipped cream or vanilla ice cream.

Sweet and Spicy Crock Pot Apple Sauce
Homemade apple sauce is the best treat ever and you can make it in a crock pot. Leave it chunky like I love to eat it or use an immersion blender to make it smooth. You can sprinkle a little cinnamon and sugar mixture over top or try some granola crumbled on top to make a desert. This recipe makes the house smell delicious.

Ingredients
8 to 10 firm apples that have been peeled, cored and sliced (I use Macintosh apples)
1/2 cup granulated sugar or use the equivalent of Splenda
1-1/2 teaspoon ground cinnamon
1/2 cup water

Directions:
1. Spray a crock pot with nonstick spray and place the peeled sliced apples in the bottom.
2. Mix the sugar and cinnamon in a bowl and sprinkle over top of the apples. Toss to coat the apple slices
3. Pour in the water
4. Cover and cook on low 6 to 8 hours or until the apples are soft. Stir every once in a while so the sugar does not burn and the apples start to break down.

Crock Pot Chocolate Nut Clusters
This recipe uses a variety of nuts including pecans, walnuts and peanuts, but you can use any combination you want. Try substituting almonds or hazelnuts for one or another of the nuts if you like. There are also three types of chocolate in the recipe. Place the clusters on wax paper to cool and pop them in candy paper cups that look like cupcake wrappers. You can also add some dried fruits to this recipe, like candied cherries or dried cranberries.

Ingredients:
3-1/2 cups toasted pecans
3-1/2 cups roasted and salted peanuts
3-1/2 cups toasted walnuts
1 – 12 ounce package of semi-sweet chocolate
1 – 12 ounce package of milk chocolate
1/4 cup powdered bittersweet chocolate or 2 ounces of solid bittersweet chocolate

Directions:
1. Spray a crock pot with nonstick spray.
2. Layer in the nuts and the chocolate.
3. Cover and cook on low for 1 hour. The chocolate should melt by then.
4. Open the lid and stir
5. Cook 2 more minutes uncovered and stir again
6. Scoop out teaspoonful's of the mixture and drop onto a cookie sheet lined with wax paper. Let it harden completely before putting in little candy cups and placing in an airtight container.

Crock Pot Chocolate Fudge
This fudge is to die for. It is creamy and it is hard to find another fudge that compares with this. You will try it once and want to make all your fudge in a crock pot from now on. Coconut milk and coconut sugar are used in the recipe and can usually be found in large supermarkets. The coconut sugar is less likely to burn in the crock pot. The fudge does have a bit of coconut flavoring, but the chocolate is what really comes through. You can also use milk chocolate chips.

Ingredients:
2-1/2 cups semi-sweet chocolate chips
1/2 cup canned coconut milk
1/4 cup coconut sugar
1 dash of sea salt
2 tablespoons coconut oil
1-1/2 teaspoon vanilla

Directions:
1. Spray a crock pot with nonstick spray.
2. Pour in the chocolate chips.
3. In a bowl combine the coconut milk, coconut sugar, salt and coconut oil. Stir it well to combine and pour over the chocolate chips
4. Place the lid on and do not take it off for 2 hours while the fudge is cooking on low.
5. Turn the crock pot off and uncover. Add the vanilla, but do not stir. Leave uncovered and let it cool. Check with a candy thermometer and once it reaches 110 degrees or cooler.

6. Use a wooden spoon and stir vigorously for about 5 to 10 minutes or until the fudge stops being glossy
7. Oil an 8 inch by 8 inch square pan and pour the fudge in. Cover and refrigerate for 4 hours or overnight. Cut in small squares. It is very rich; you don't need a big square.

Conclusion

I hope you have found inspiration on using that crock pot or slow cooker that sits in your closet. Crock pots and slow cookers are a must have appliance for every kitchen. You can make everything from main dishes to appetizers and desserts with them. They are very versatile. It is hard to burn anything in them and almost always, the recipe turns out good. The best thing about it is there is rarely any muss or fuss. You just pour the ingredients in and let them go for a time. You can even cook while you are at work with a slow cooker or crock pot and sit down to eat within minutes of arriving at home.

Use your crock pot for family meals or for parties. You can even serve your dishes right out of the crock pot set on the table for a pot luck dinner. The nice thing about slow cooking is that it retains flavor and moisture in a recipe much better than using the oven where liquids and flavors evaporate. I guarantee that the Swiss steak you make in a Dutch oven on the stove will never taste as delicious as the one you make in your crock pot.

If you do not have a crock pot or slow cooker, check out this video entitled, "Crock Pot Questions" by KUTV2NEWS in an interview with Karen Petersen, another crock pot cookbook author. It will help you make a decision on which one to buy, how to clean and how to solve some problems that might come up in using a crock pot or slow cooker.

Need more recipes? Here is a video that will give you more. "20 Easy Crockpot Recipes in 4 Ingredients or Less" by PopSugar food will expand your recipe box even more.

I hope this book was able to help you to use your crock pot or slow cooker to its fullest abilities.

The next step is to set up that slow cooker or crock pot and start cooking.

Finally, if you discovered at least one thing that has helped you or that you think would be beneficial to someone else, be sure to take a few seconds to easily post a quick positive review. As an author, your positive feedback is desperately needed. Your highly valuable five star reviews are like a river of golden joy flowing through a sunny forest of mighty trees and beautiful flowers! *To do your good deed in making the world a better place by helping others with your valuable insight, just leave a nice review.*

My Other Books and Audio Books
www.AcesEbooks.com

Popular Books

Be sure to check out my audio books as well!

Check out my website at: **www.AcesEbooks.com** for a complete list of all of my books and high quality audio books. I enjoy bringing you the best knowledge in the world and wish you the best in using this information to make your journey through life better and more enjoyable! **Best of luck to you!**

www.ingramcontent.com/pod-product-compliance
Lightning Source LLC
LaVergne TN
LVHW080845090225
803299LV00012B/1274